JUG BANDS AND HANDMADE MUSIC
A Creative Approach To Music Theory and the Instruments

Other Books on Music by James Lincoln Collier

PRACTICAL MUSIC THEORY: HOW MUSIC IS PUT TOGETHER FROM
　　　BACH TO ROCK
WHICH MUSICAL INSTRUMENT SHALL I PLAY? (with Yale Joel)
INSIDE JAZZ

Other Books by James Lincoln Collier

IT'S MURDER AT ST. BASKET'S
THE TEDDY BEAR HABIT
WHY DOES EVERYBODY THINK I'M NUTTY?
DANNY GOES TO THE HOSPITAL (with Yale Joel)
A VISIT TO THE FIREHOUSE (with Yale Joel)
BATTLEGROUND: THE UNITED STATES NAVY IN WORLD WAR II

JUG BANDS AND HANDMADE MUSIC

A Creative Approach To Music Theory and the Instruments

by James Lincoln Collier

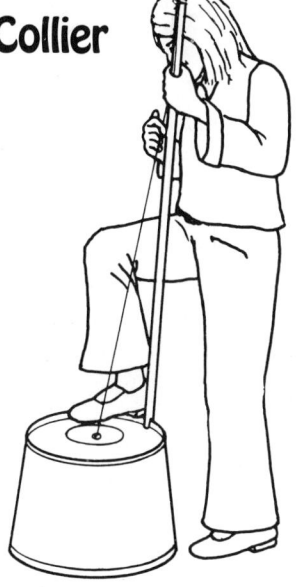

A THISTLE BOOK
Published by
GROSSET & DUNLAP, INC.
A National General Company
New York

Copyright © 1973 by James Lincoln Collier
"Unemployment Blues" Copyright © 1973 by James Lincoln Collier
"Turkey Blues" Copyright © 1973 by James Lincoln Collier
"Frogtown Rock" Copyright © 1973 by Geoffrey Lincoln Collier
Photo credits; p. 7, 8, Ludwig Drum Company
                p. 33, Scherl & Roth, Inc.
All Rights Reserved
Published Simultaneously in Canada
Library of Congress Catalog Card No. 73-4457
ISBN: 0-448-26248-7 (library edition)

Printed in the United States of America

For Bronwen, Maggie and Alexander

Contents

	Introduction	1
1	Making Drums and Rhythm	3
2	Writing Music Down	13
3	The Heartbeat of Music	21
4	Pitches, Notes and Guitars	29
5	Notes That Make Melodies	37
6	Writing Melodies	44
7	Making a Guitar—and Chords for It	56
8	More Chords—and More Strings	67
9	Making Wind Instruments	79
10	Some Other Instruments	89
11	The Modern Sound—Electronic Instruments	94
12	Putting Your Jug Band Together	101
	Appendix: Music for Your Jug Band	105
	Index	113

Introduction

Most people everywhere in the world love music. They like to listen to it, they like to dance to it, but the thing they like best is making it themselves. In some places almost everybody is a musician. And this is getting to be true of the United States. Americans buy a quarter of a million pianos, a half million wind instruments, two and a half million guitars every year. In almost half of our families somebody plays something. Everywhere, people are anxious to learn to play something, even if it is a relatively simple instrument like the harmonica, millions of which are sold every year. People just plain like making music.

This book is about making homemade musical instruments. Most of the ones I have included you can really make in a few minutes, once you have learned the trick. You can make them in your own home with a few friends, or in a classroom with your schoolmates. If you are willing to work at it a bit, you will end up with enough instruments to make up a real band which can play real music.

Bands of homemade instruments are often called "jug bands," for reasons you will eventually discover in this book. Jug bands have existed for a long time in the United States, especially in the poor country areas where nobody had enough money to buy real instruments. Today a lot of young people are organizing jug bands just for fun.

As I have said, this book is about making homemade instruments; but really it is about music. As you go along making your instruments, you will discover what music is and how it works. You will learn how the different families of instruments—the strings, the winds, the percussion—make their notes and why they sound different. (It is more correct to speak of the 'tone' a musical instrument makes, but 'note' is the more commonly used word and I have used it in this book.) You will learn a little bit about reading music, a little bit about scales and chords—because in order to play music you have to know something about these things. You will, finally, learn how to write your own songs for your own jug band.

In the process, you will begin to get some idea of which types of instruments you like best and enjoy playing the most. In time, you may decide to take up a real instrument, and your experience with these homemade instruments will not only have given you a start, but helped you decide what kind of instrument you want to play.

But even if you don't take up a real instrument, your experience with your jug band will give you some understanding of music. Understanding music makes it far more enjoyable. And that, of course, is what it is really all about: first of all music is for pleasure.

1
Making Drums and Rhythm

Music is sound. But it is not any sound; it is a special kind of sound. The voices of people talking, the noise a truck makes when it rumbles by, the slam of a door or barking of a dog—these kinds of sounds are not generally considered music. What makes the difference? What makes sound, anyway?

Sound is produced when something vibrates—that is to say, moves rapidly back and forth. You can see many things around you that vibrate. In fact, anything that is making a sound is vibrating, although you can't usually see it. But hold a ruler at one end firmly against a desk or table, and snap the other end, like this:

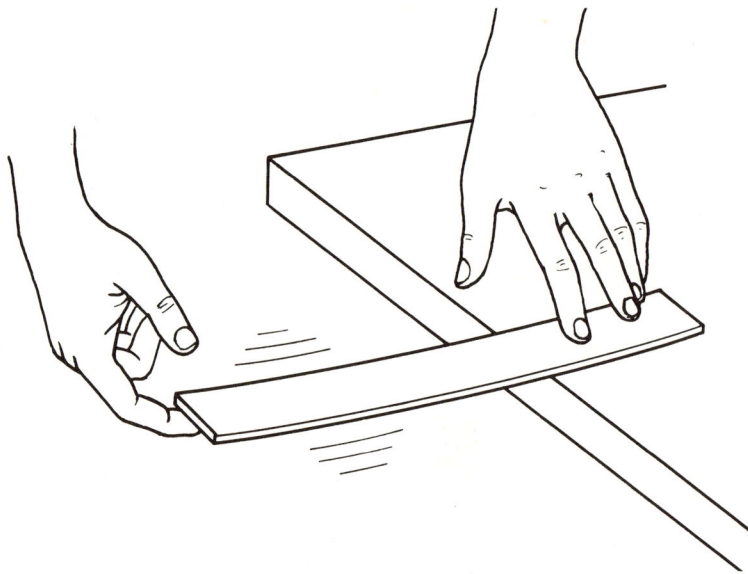

You can clearly see it vibrate, and you will also notice that as long as it is vibrating it is making a sound. Or have somebody stretch a rubber band with his hands, and snap one side of it; you can see it vibrate and you can hear it hum. You can do this by yourself by stretching the rubber band across the back of a chair, like this:

Or hold a pot lid in the air with one hand and touch the edge lightly with a fingernail. If somebody gives it a tap with a spoon or a pencil, you will be able to feel it vibrate, and you will hear a ringing sound. (You need a fairly heavy lid for this—the thin, light ones do not vibrate very well.)

Through these experiments you can actually see musical sounds being made. What is the difference, then, between these sounds and the other sounds like the rumbling of trucks and the barking of dogs that we call noise? The difference is this: in musical sounds, the vibrations are regular, each one coming along the same fraction of a second after the one before it. If you could draw it, it would look like this:

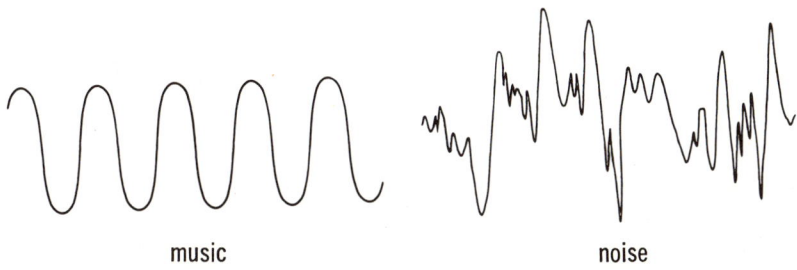

music   noise

In noise, the vibrations are of different lengths, with lots of different kinds jumbled together at once. In a sense, a musical sound is a kind of simple, regular noise. To give an example, if you take your pencil and draw a lot of lines and dots helter-skelter, you have just a bunch of lines; but if you organize the lines and dots some way, you have a design. Similarly, music is "organized" sound.

Music is different in different parts of the world. The music of African peoples, for example, does not have very much "melody" to it in our sense of the word, but it is far more complicated than our music in terms of rhythm. We generally find it difficult to understand, just as the people who play it often find our music very odd. But despite these differences, music is really a universal human language. People everywhere use the same basic ideas in organizing it.

Perhaps the most fundamental of all ways of organizing music is rhythm. It is virtually impossible to make music which does not have rhythm, although there are a few kinds that get away from a regular rhythm. But most people prefer music with rhythm. As a matter of fact, most people like music with strong, definite rhythms, especially if they are going to dance to it.

This is not surprising, because rhythm is fundamental to all life. Our hearts beat in rhythm, we run or walk in rhythm, we breathe in rhythm. There is a natural rhythm to the seasons, a rhythm to the tides, a rhythm to the movements of the sun and moon and stars. Even before man was civilized he loved rhythm; there are still preserved in the hardened mud at the bottom of a cave in Europe the footprints of a boy who danced there thousands of years ago.

Rhythm is so much a part of our natures that it is easy to see why it is so basic to music. One of the first things we notice when we listen to any kind of music, from rock to Christmas carols, is the beat. Almost without thinking of it, you begin to beat time with your feet. How do you know when to tap? In other words, how do you know where the beat is? The music itself tells you. You can *feel* the beat because it is tied right into the notes themselves.

Music, I have said, is organized sound. And one way we organize it is to divide it into those beats you feel when you tap your feet.

In much music, although not all, there are certain instruments which are given the job of marking out those beats as they come along. These are the percussion instruments, or the percussion "family" as we say. The term percussion comes from the Latin word for "to beat," and that should immediately give you a clue as to what instruments belong to this family. You are undoubtedly familiar with them. There are those cymbals you hear clashing in marching bands, those big kettledrums found in all orchestras, the complete drum "sets" in rock bands, and a host of gongs, triangles, chimes, rattles and many more. As a matter of fact, your own body can be a percussion instrument as when you clap your hands, stomp your feet or even slap your hands on your chest or thighs. Here are some of the most important percussion instruments:

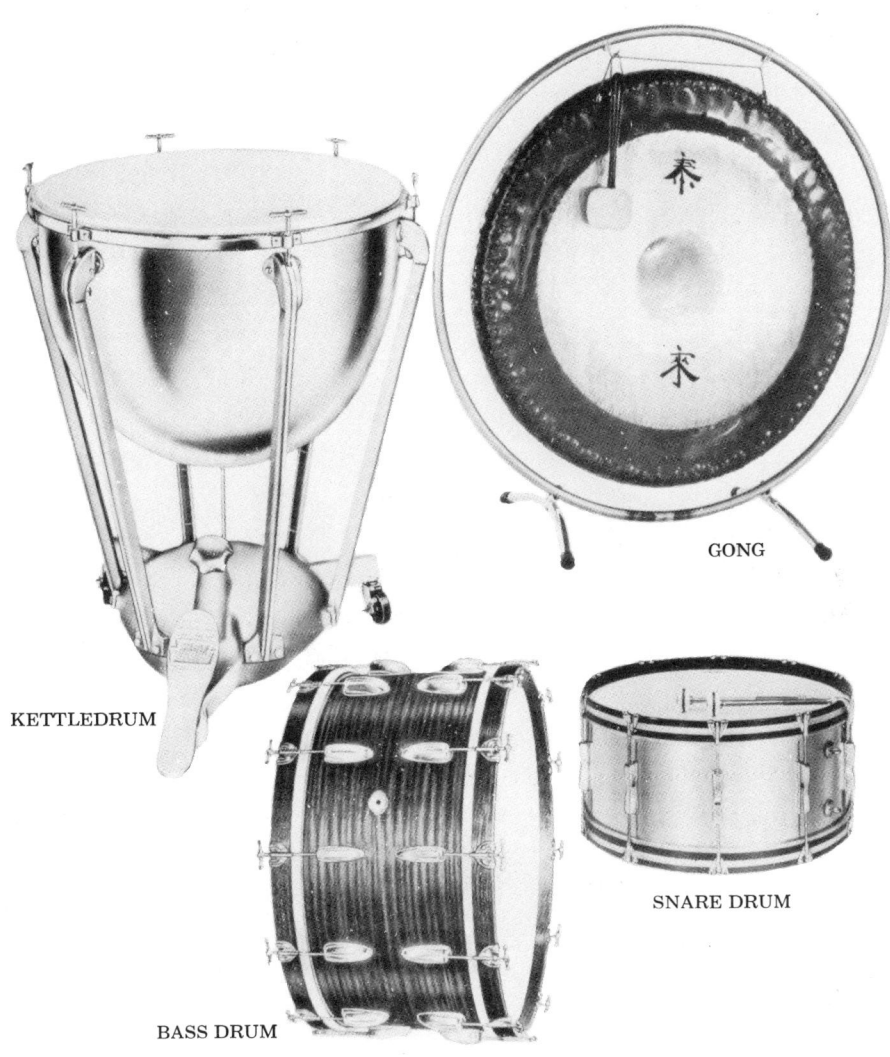

KETTLEDRUM

GONG

BASS DRUM

SNARE DRUM

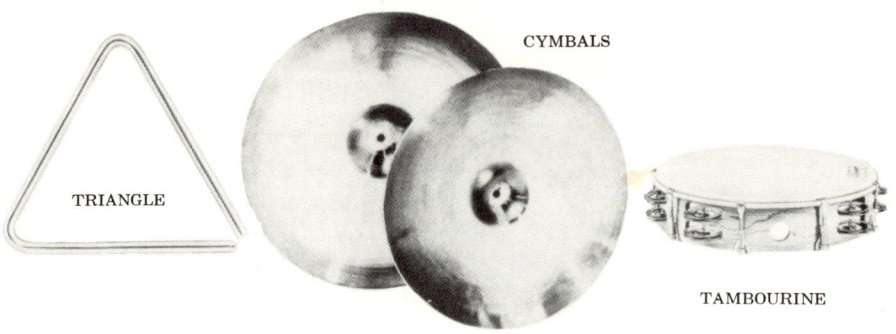

It is very easy to make percussion instruments for your jug band out of things that you can find around the house. A pot lid, especially the heavy-duty kind, makes a great cymbal if you bang on it with the back of a spoon. But hold it by the handle, or if you like, dangle it from a string tied to the knob. You will notice that if you hold the lid by the metal it makes a much duller sound than if you hold it by the knob. This is because when your hand is on the metal it prevents the metal from vibrating as well as it might. Your own imagination will suggest other kinds of things that will make good cymbals or gongs.

Other kinds of percussion instruments widely used are the shakers or rattles. Put some dried peas or a few pieces of macaroni in a Bandaid box—the metal kind, not the cardboard ones. Again, your imagination will suggest dozens of other ways of making rattles. Experiment with various types of containers and rattles until you discover the ones that make the sounds you like best. (If you use glass containers, make sure they are strong enough not to break.)

Another percussion instrument you can make in about one minute is an embroidery hoop tambourine. An embroidery hoop is a device for stretching a piece of cloth tightly so that designs can be sewn into it. It consists of two hoops, one inside of the other. The outside hoop can be drawn up tightly against the inside one by means of a screw you turn with your fingers. You can buy an embroidery hoop at a five-and-ten-cent store for less than a dollar. Instead of putting cloth in it, put in a sheet of plastic, like this:

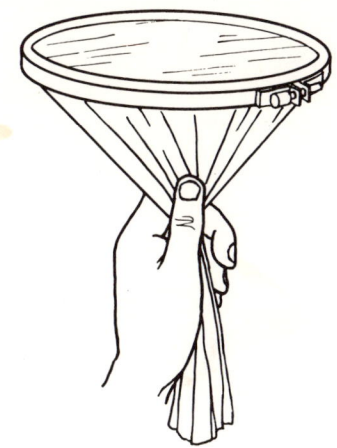

Have somebody pull the plastic as tight as possible while you tighten the screws. The tighter you stretch the plastic, the better sound you will get.

Yet another kind of percussion instrument is one that is not exactly struck, but is scraped—although when you scrape a stick across something rough you are actually "striking" all the little rough spots. Paste some sandpaper on two ordinary wood blocks or any pieces of wood and simply rub them together. Or cut small notches in a pencil or piece of dowling, and scrape it with something metal. A large table knife or spoon, especially a silver one, will give a pleasant ringing sound when used as a scraper:

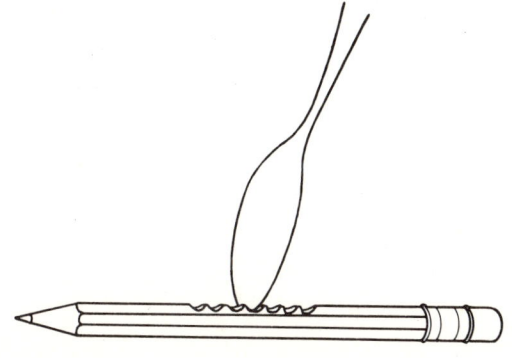

Finally, there is the most popular of all percussion instruments, the drum. And this brings us to an important principle in music-making, the principle of resonance. To get an idea of how the principle of resonance works, get a pot or heavy glass or bowl or anything similar, and stretch a rubber band across the top like this:

When you snap it, you will notice how much louder and more musical it sounds than when you simply hold it between your hands and snap it. This is because the rubber band is not vibrating alone: it is making the glass or pot and the air inside it vibrate too, which adds to the sound. The sound is being "amplified"—that is, made larger.

The scientific law that makes the principle of resonance work says that if you vibrate something which is attached to something else, the something else will vibrate as well. Resonance is employed in most of our important musical instruments. We start by vibrating something small, because it is much easier to get the kind of vibration we want in a small thing than in a large one. The small thing is attached to the large, and makes it resonate, amplifying the sound. A perfect example is a guitar or violin string. A guitar string by itself makes a very tiny sound, one that you can hardly hear unless you are close. But when it is attached to a guitar, it makes not only the wood of the guitar, but the air inside the guitar, vibrate, too, amplifying the sound. Similarly the strings inside a piano are attached to a huge piece of wood called the sounding board, which resonates when the strings are struck. In a somewhat more complicated way, the wind instruments like trumpets, flutes and French horns are basically devices for amplifying vibrations made when a jet of air passes through a narrow opening. (When we get to the wind family you will find out more about how this works.)

A drum employs the principle of resonance, too. It is basically a device for amplifying the vibrations made when you tap a tightly stretched sheet of membrane. For thousands of years, until very recently, drumheads were invariably made of animal skins. Even today many drumheads are still made of cowhide. However, since the invention of synthetic materials, more and more drumheads are being made of plastic. And this gives us a very easy way to make a whole variety of drums. Get some plastic garbage bags of various sizes. There are big ones for trash containers, smaller ones for garbage cans. Then get some bowls, sturdy glasses, pails or wastebaskets. It is better if the tops are perfectly round, without spouts or handles to get in the way. Put a plastic bag over each container, like this:

Now gather the plastic together under the bottom of the container, like this:

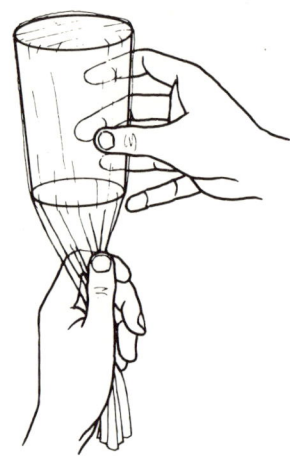

and twist it until the top is smooth and quite tight. Tap it with something, and you'll discover you have a drum. The back of a spoon makes a good beater because it will not punch holes in the drumhead.

You can probably manage to hold a little drum the size of a glass and play it yourself at the same time, but for bigger drums made out of bowls or pails, you may need to work in teams of two or three, with some people holding while one person drums. The important thing is to get the head as smooth and as tight as you can. The spoon should bounce off the head pretty easily when you hit it.

Now, use your imagination and see how many percussion instruments you can invent for your jug band. When you see bands on television or in your school, pay special attention to the percussion instruments to see how they sound and how they are played. These real instruments can give you some good ideas for your own homemade ones.

2
Writing Music Down

You now have a band—at least, you have a rhythm band. You can't play any songs or melodies with this band, but you can play rhythms—as many fascinating and exciting kinds of rhythms as you can think up. And this brings us again to the point made in the last chapter about music being organized sound. Try letting everybody bang away on their instruments in any way they want without paying any attention to the other people. It may be fun at first, but it gets pretty boring after a while. This is because anything that is totally disorganized gets tiresome in time. So we must find a way to organize our rhythms. And one device that we will find most helpful for this purpose is musical notation.

"Musical notation" is a phrase which means the way you write notes down on paper for musicians to read. It is a very useful thing to know how to read music. If you compose a song, you will be able to remember it exactly the next time you want to play it, if you can write it down on paper. Or you can give it to your friend to play. Or you can write down music for the members of a band so that the parts go together properly. And of course, if you can read music, you can play all the thousands upon thousands of pieces that have been written down by other composers. Learning to read music takes time, and it is not always easy, but you can learn quite a bit very quickly if you put a little effort into it.

You will remember that music is sound organized into beats coming along one after another, usually at the same speed. In writing down music there are several ways of indicating a single beat. One of the commonest of all symbols for one beat is the quarter note:

♩

Actually, in musical notation a quarter note can be made to stand for two beats or half a beat or even several beats. We will get into that in a little while, but for now let us think of a quarter note as standing for one beat. Thus, if you write down a row of quarter notes, you are indicating a number of regular beats. Try playing this line of notes a few times by tapping them out with a pencil:

But how do you know how fast to play those quarter notes? The only way to know is if there is a special sign or symbol at the beginning of the music to tell you. These signs are often Italian words like *lento,* which means "slow," or *presto,* which means "very fast;" but don't worry about this now. The speed at which you play is called the "tempo"; if there isn't any tempo marking, you can decide for yourself how fast to play.

A second most important sign is this one:

It is called a "quarter rest." It means just what it says—rest, don't play. You can say that it stands for a gap in the music exactly one beat long. If you want, you can think of it as telling you to skip that beat. Suppose you come upon this:

It means to play every other beat, and leave every other beat out. Practice it a few times by beating all the beats with your foot and tapping just the quarter notes with your pencil.

Now that you have got the idea of rests, you can quickly see that you can make up all sorts of combinations of quarter notes and quarter rests to organize your music in an interesting way. Here is one way. As you can see, you play one beat and then skip the next two:

Here is still another way:

There a great many ways of combining quarter notes and quarter rests. And you don't have to be regular, either:

Obviously, there are hundreds of combinations of quarter notes and quarter rests that you can work out.

So now you can see one way of organizing music that makes it interesting and exciting—that makes it "sound good." But that is only a beginning. If you think about it for a minute, you can see that all the players in the band don't have to play the same notes. Each player can have different notes. As you know already if you have listened to much music, composers switch the music around a lot, giving the melodies to different instruments, and changing the backgrounds, too. You can undoubtedly find records to listen to which will show you examples of this.

And, of course, you can do the same thing with your rhythm band. Here are two little pieces of music. Have the drums play the line on the top and all the other instruments the one on the bottom. As you can see immediately, the drums play while the other instruments rest, and vice versa:

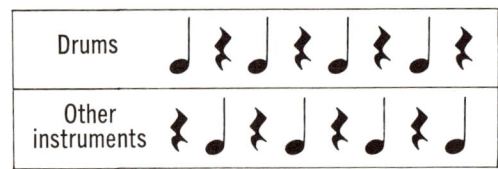

Now try it the other way around:

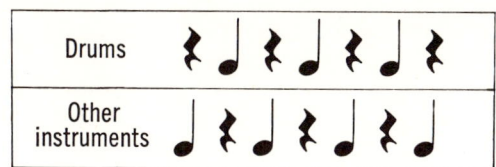

Here is another combination that makes an interesting sound:

You can divide your band into three groups instead of two. Have the drums play one part, the cymbals another and the rest of the instruments the third:

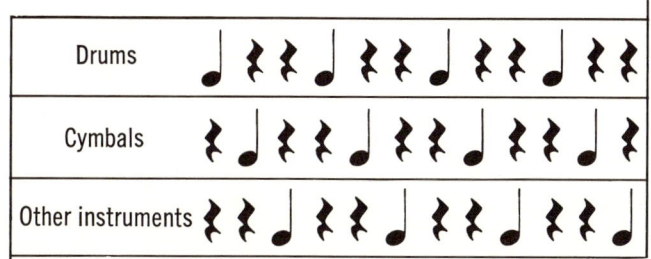

Here is another way to divide up the parts. You will notice that the drums play with the cymbals only on certain notes. That is to make those particular notes stand out and seem stronger:

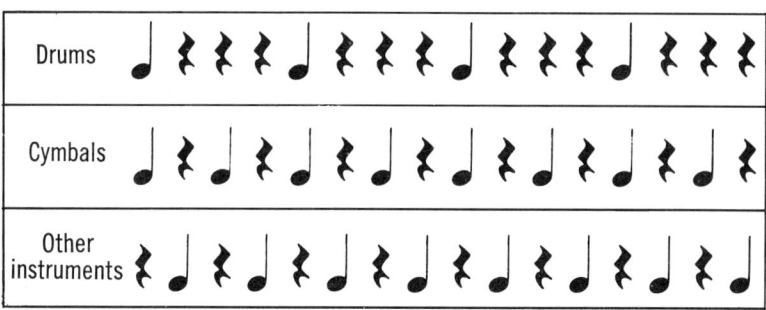

The last example is included for a particular reason, because it demonstrates something else about how we organize music. Play it again a couple of times, and notice how the beats seem to belong in clusters of four. That is to say, the first four beats sound as if they make up one group, the second four beats a second group and so on. In order to make this a little clearer I'll give you the same example again, only this time with lines dividing it into these four-beat groups:

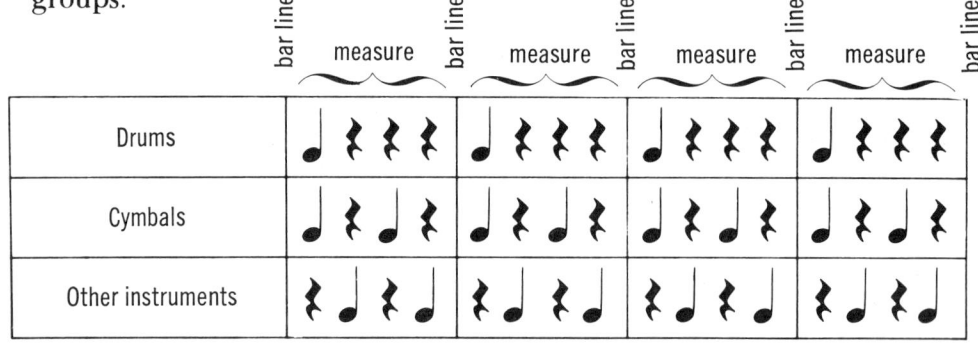

The reason why this music seems to divide itself up like this is because the drums emphasize the note at the beginning of each group.

So here is the point. We have seen that music is organized into beats; now we can see that in most music the beats themselves are organized into groups of beats. We call these groups measures, or sometimes "bars" of music, because they are divided by lines or "bars" as I have done in the preceding example. Here is a bit from a hymn called "Faith of Our Fathers" in which you can easily see the bar lines. You can also tell without much trouble how many beats are clustered in each bar, or measure, to stick with the usual term:

Faith of Our Fathers

A measure of music can contain as many beats as you want. However, in most of the music you ordinarily hear, the measures contain two, three, or four beats. Occasionally you come across music with six or eight beats to the measure. However, you can make your measures as long as you want—fifty beats long if you like. Anything is possible. In the dance music of a few centuries ago they often used nine- and twelve-beat bars. Modern composers sometimes write measures that are one, five, and seven beats long. Jazz players also occasionally use five- and seven-beat measures. In fact, they are today experimenting with measures containing three and a half beats and other odd combinations. Moreover, it is quite possible to mix measures of various lengths together, so that you have, say, a few three-beat measures popping up here and there among a lot of four-beat measures.

As you can see, you can make your measures anything you like. In composing for your band you might want to experiment, but obviously you will find the more usual ones, like two-, three-, and four-beat measures more familiar to your ear.

3
The Heartbeat of Music

You are now beginning to understand something about the way music is organized. You have seen that it is divided into beats, and that the beats can be collected into measures of various lengths. Now you will see that even though all those beats coming along one after another look the same on paper, they do not sound the same. Some of them are more important, or "stronger" than others. They seem to emphasize themselves more. Invariably, the first beat in a measure is the strongest. In a two-beat measure it goes:

In a three-beat measure it is:

Four-beat measures work a little differently. The first note is still the strongest beat in the measure; but the third note is a strong one, too, although not quite as strong as the first one. So in a four-beat measure we have this:

The reason why certain beats are stronger than others is probably obvious to you. The first in a row of anything always stands out the most just because it is first. And the third beat in that four-beat measure seems strong, too, because it is the beginning of the second half of the measure. In the same way, in a six-beat measure the first beat will be the strongest, but the fourth beat will be strong, too, because it is the beginning of the second half of the measure:

Now you can put the strong and weak beats to use in your music. Here is one way to do it:

As you can see, the cymbals are emphasizing the strong beats in a four-beat measure. Now write down your own experiments with strong beats in two- or three-beat measures—or any kind of measures you want.

But there is another way of dealing with these strong and weak beats. What happens when you emphasize the *weak* beats rather than the strong ones?

Cymbals	𝄽 ♩ 𝄽 ♩	𝄽 ♩ 𝄽 ♩	𝄽 ♩ 𝄽 ♩
All others	♩♩♩♩	♩♩♩♩	♩♩♩♩

Emphasizing the weak beats instead of the strong ones gives the music a somewhat odd feeling, a little bit as if it were going backwards. Nonetheless it is an effect familiar to you. Jazz music has always used a great deal of this "off-beat" emphasis. Because jazz has influenced a great deal of our popular music, you can hear this effect often in much of the music you hear.

We have seen how beats can be added together to make measures of music. But if we can *add* beats, we also ought to be able to divide them. And that is exactly what we can do. A half of a quarter note is called an eighth note, and it is written like this:

Two halves make a whole, so two eighth notes equal one quarter note. When you have two eighth notes next to each other they are sometimes tied together, like this:

$$♪♪ = ♫$$

So now you know that:

$$♫ = ♩$$

And of course if there are four quarter notes in a measure there will be eight eighth notes. Let's see how that works out in practice:

Often, when you have many eighth notes coming along in a row one after another like that, they are tied together in groups of four. Try it again, only switching the parts:

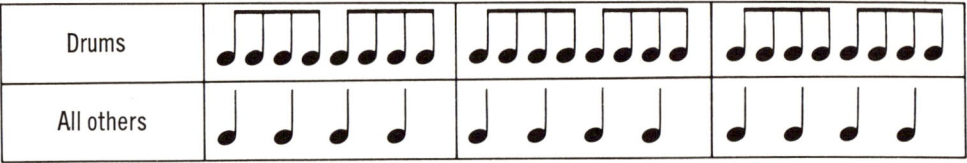

You can probably guess that anything you can do with quarter notes you can do with eighth notes, too. You can emphasize certain ones if you want, and you can leave some of them out. The sign for an eighth-note rest, or eighth rest as we usually call it, is this:

7

Now let's see what happens when you leave a few eighth notes out. Separate yourselves into three groups: drums and two other groups with the instruments more or less equally divided. Now try this:

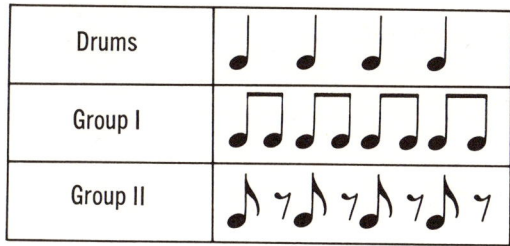

Switch the groups around so everybody has a chance at all the parts. Perhaps you can feel that we are again dealing with that problem of emphasis. The first *beat* in a measure is strong because it is the beginning. In the same way the first *half* of a beat is also the strongest half, because it is also the beginning. This means, of course, that the first of two eighth notes is the strongest. And in the little piece of music you have just been playing, you were emphasizing that strong first eighth note because Group II was only playing that one and leaving the second one blank.

But just as you can switch the emphasis onto the weak beats in a measure to get a special effect, so can you switch the emphasis onto the second half of the beat for a special effect. You do this by playing only the *second* of the two eighth notes that make up a quarter note. This idea of emphasizing the second half of any beat is called syncopation. It is one of the basic characteristics of jazz, and it is very common in other kinds of popular music, too, especially rock. Here is an example of syncopation:

Drums	♩ ♩ ♩ ♩
Group I	♫ ♫ ♫ ♫
Group II	𝄾♪ 𝄾♪ 𝄾♪ 𝄾♪

Try that one a few times, switching the groups around, until everybody gets the idea. You want to make sure that everybody has it right, because this next one coming up is even tougher, since the eighth notes are not being marked out.

Drums	♩ ♩ ♩ ♩	♩ ♩ ♩ ♩
All others	𝄾♪ 𝄾♪ 𝄾♪ 𝄾♪	𝄾♪ 𝄾♪ 𝄾♪ 𝄾♪

You should already be able to get the idea you can mix up quarter notes, eighth notes, quarter rests, and eighth rests any way you want to in order to put interesting rhythms in your music. As a matter of fact, each eighth note can be divided further into two sixteenth notes, and each sixteenth note into two thirty-second notes and so on, although thirty-second notes and the ones beyond are pretty rare. These notes are written like this:

They are also tied together in groups:

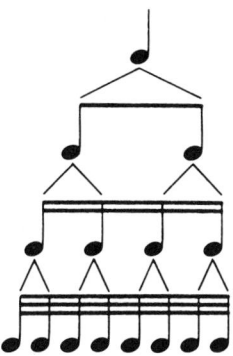

To begin with, I would advise you to stick with quarter notes and eighth notes. You can make up many hundreds, even thousands of interesting combinations out of them without bothering with sixteenths and so forth. Experiment on your own: here are some ideas to get you started:

28

4
Pitches, Notes and Guitars

Rhythm is one way of organizing music. But there are other ways of organizing it, too. Next to rhythm the most important is *pitch*. Pitch is the word that means how high or low a note is. The notes that a little bird sings are pitched high. The roaring of a tiger is low pitched.

What gives a note its particular pitch? Why is one note higher than another? You can discover the answer by having another look at a vibrating rubber band. In the first chapter you stretched a rubber band across something and watched it vibrate. Now try it again, but this time as you pluck it stretch the rubber band. Notice that the pitch immediately rises.

Here's why. As you know, the difference between a noise and a musical note is that in the musical note the vibrations are regular, in the noise they are not. That is to say, whatever is making the musical sound—the rubber band, for example—is flying back and forth at a constant rate. It might make fifty vibrations per second; it might make 5,000; but the vibrations are regular.

The faster something vibrates, the higher the pitch. The speed of a note's vibration is called its frequency. A note with a frequency of, say, 440 vibrations per second sounds a higher pitch than one vibrating at a frequency of 300, or even 439, although you certainly couldn't hear any difference between pitches vibrating at frequencies that close together.

Just as a matter of interest, most people can't hear notes with frequencies below about 30 vibrations per second: the notes are too low to hear. Similarly, we don't hear notes with frequencies above 15,000 very well, either, although some people, especially children with their sharper ears, can hear frequencies up to around 20,000. You may have heard about whistles that dogs can hear but people can't. This happens because dogs can hear higher frequencies than human beings; the whistle is pitched too high for humans, but still at frequencies a dog can hear.

The next question, of course, is what gives anything its pitch—that is, why does it vibrate at that particular frequency? It has to do with the material it is made of. The subject is too complicated to go into in this book, but you can see the truth of it by banging some pot lids, or tapping glasses or drumheads with something. Notice that no matter what you tap it with, the pitch produced by the pot lid or glass always remains the same. If you hit it with the eraser end of a pencil the sound will be a lot softer and more delicate than if you hit it with a spoon; but the *pitch* will always be the same.

Now how does this explain why the rubber band goes up in pitch when you stretch it? Simply because when you stretch a rubber band, you are actually "changing" the material it is made of. A stretched rubber band is harder and more resilient than a limp one; as you "change" the material, the pitch changes, too. And you can see how sensitive pitch is to change; you don't have to stretch your rubber band very much to make the pitch rise.

Whatever a thing is made of, thus, has an effect on its pitch. But there is a second quality that helps determine pitch; and that is the *size* of a thing. In general, the smaller anything is the faster it will vibrate when struck or plucked. And, of course, the faster it vibrates, the higher the pitch will be.

You can easily prove this for yourself. Stretch a rubber band over the back of a chair. Take it between your thumb and fingers somewhere down toward one end, and pluck the longer section of it. You will notice that the rubber band does not vibrate beyond your fingers, in the shorter section.

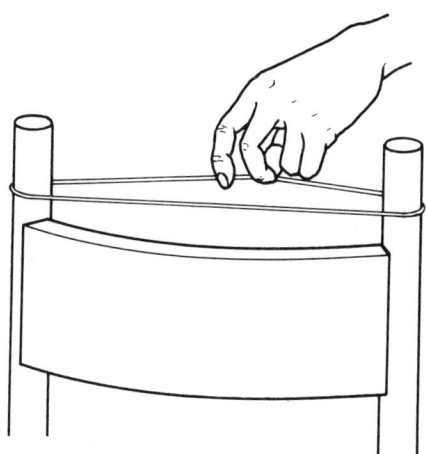

You are shortening the string by holding it. Now slide your fingers along the band to shorten it even more, and keep plucking it as you slide. As you can readily tell, the pitch rises as the vibrating part of the rubber band gets shorter.

The thin, short strings on the piano make the high notes; the long, fat ones make the low notes. Small musical instruments like flutes and trumpets usually play higher than big ones like tubas and bassoons. You can check this out by testing different sizes of pot lids (of course, they have to be the same type of pot lid) or better yet, with drums. But there is an even better experiment to do which will not only show you how pitches are made, but will introduce you to a second family of instruments, the strings.

For the past several hundred years strings have been the most important of our musical families. The violin, especially, and its larger cousins, the viola, violoncello (more often called 'cello) and string bass, have been at the heart of most classical music. At one time they were also the main instruments in dance bands, country bands and many others. In the past hundred years or so, great improvements have been made in wind instruments like trumpets and clarinets, making them easier to play than they used to be, and they have risen in popularity at the expense of the strings. But the string family still contains the richest and most versatile of our instruments.

The stringed instrument you are most familiar with, however, is undoubtedly the guitar. A hundred years ago the guitar was a rare instrument; today, due to the popularity of jazz, folk music, rock and the blues, the guitar is second only to the piano in popularity in the United States. The guitar has a number of cousins: the mandolin, the banjo, ukelele, the Russian balalaika, the Indian sitar and a host of others. Ancient peoples used to make a stringed instrument by snapping a bowstring. If you hold a bow upright, with one end on the ground, you can change the pitch by pressing down on it. When you press, the bow bends slightly and the string is a bit less taut.

There are a number of differences between these various stringed instruments, which I will get into later in the book, but for a beginning, you can make a stringed instrument of your own.

If you have ever seen a stringed instrument like a violin or bass you will remember that the strings aren't simply tacked onto a board. Instead, they are attached to a kind of hollow box of a special shape made of quite thin wood.

VIOLIN

VIOLA

CELLO

BASS

A plucked string makes a rather quiet sound. But if you attach it to something larger, it will make that vibrate, too. In a stringed instrument, the "box" part vibrates along with the string, and so does the air inside of it. They "resonate" along with the string and amplify its sound to make it louder.

It is quite simple to turn your rubber band into a real stringed instrument by attaching it to a resonator. For this you need a box. A wooden box, especially one made of thin wood like a cigar box, is best because wood resonates especially well. However, a cardboard shoe box will do nicely and may be easier to get. Because you may eventually need several, I suggest you work with shoe boxes in the beginning. If you can't get any, at most five-and-tens you can buy plastic food boxes about the size of shoe boxes for about fifty cents each.

Besides your box and a heavy duty rubber band, you need a ruler, some tape, a couple of small blocks of wood, approximately an inch square and a half an inch or so thick, and some glue—ordinary white glue will do fine. Your first step is to tape up the box where the top fits on, like this:

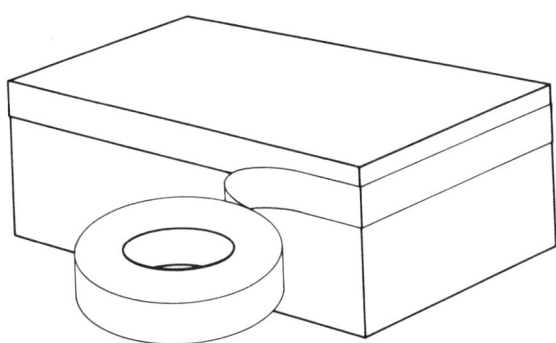

If the box has any holes, tears or cracks you should seal them up, too. Now glue the blocks of wood and the ruler to the top of the box like this:

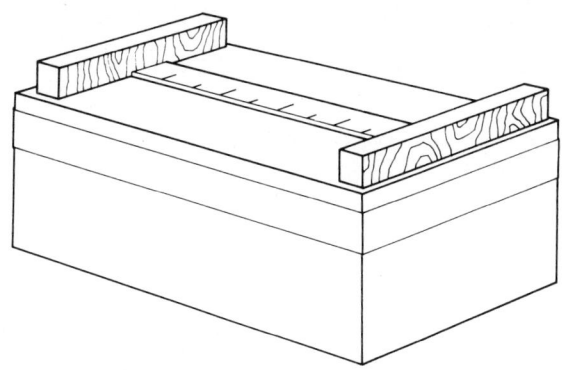

If you are using a plastic box it is a good idea to roughen the surface with a bit of sandpaper to make the glue hold better. It is also important to put some kind of weight on the blocks and the ruler while the glue is drying. If the ruler is too long for your box, saw some off one end to make it fit.

It will take the white glue about two hours or so to dry. Now put your rubber band completely around the box and over the blocks, like this:

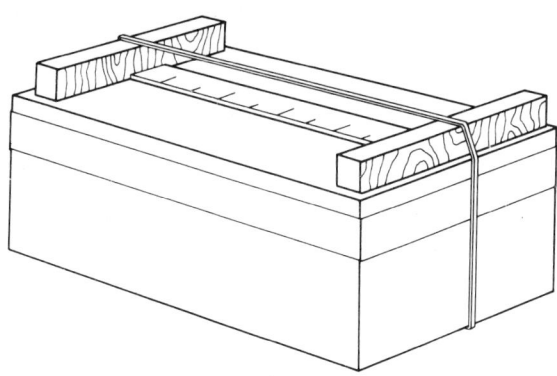

Your resonator is now complete. What you have, in fact, is a stringed instrument, on which you can play tunes once you have had a bit of practice. To play it, hold a piece of wood like a ruler on the string lightly touching it, like this:

You can pluck the string with your finger, but it is a little easier to pluck it with a paperclip or a coin. By sliding the ruler from place to place you shorten or lengthen your rubber band and raise or lower the pitch. This ruler is called a "movable bridge."

5
Notes That Make Melodies

At this point you need to know how to produce any given pitch on your rubber band. You already know how to do this with your voice. Have somebody play a note on a piano, or a pitch pipe—in fact, on anything. Then sing the same note. If you have had much experience in singing you will be able to do this easily; if you haven't, you may make a few wrong tries before you get it.

Now let's try to do the same thing on your homemade stringed instrument. I am going to suggest that you start with the note C, for reasons that I will explain later in this book. If there's a piano available you can easily find a C. Notice that the black notes on the piano come in groups of two and three. The white key immediately below any group of *two* black notes is *always* a C:

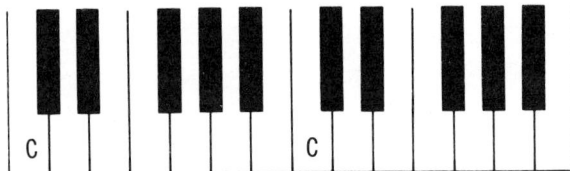

The other white keys are named after the letters of the alphabet like this:

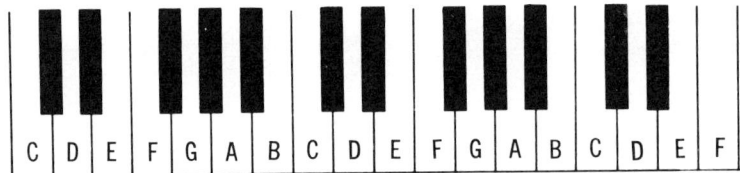

The black keys are named for the white keys next to them. A black key above a white key is called a sharp, below a white key a flat. Thus, the black key above D is called D sharp, normally written D♯; the black key below D is called D flat, written D♭. As you can see, the black keys have white keys on both sides of them. Which one do they take their name from? Both, actually. The black key between C and D can be called either C♯, because it is *above* C, or D♭, because it is *below* D.

If you have no piano available, you can get a C from a pitch pipe, or from some other musical instrument. First sing it a few times to get it clearly in your mind. Then start sliding your movable bridge along the rubber band as you pluck it, until you find the C. This will not be easy at first, but with a little practice you will get the trick. After you have found the C, slide your bridge an inch or so away, and then back until you hit the C again. Do this a number of times until it comes easily.

Once you have got the C worked out, experiment with a few other notes. Probably the most important thing you can do to improve your musical ability is to practice finding a few notes, both on the rubber band, and by singing, every day. If you want to learn to play basketball you must practice hook shots and jump shots over and over. If you want to play music, you need to develop your ability to hit notes just the way you hit the basket with the basketball. This is called ear training. The more accurate your ear becomes, the easier anything concerning music will be for you.

Once you have found the C, make a note of where it is on the pasted-down ruler. Next, cut a small block of wood high enough to just fit between the rubber band and the top of the box. The block should touch the string firmly. It doesn't matter if it raises it up a little:

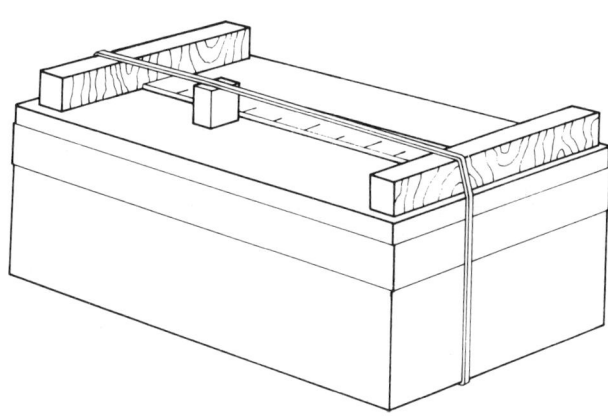

Place the block where you have found the C. Play C again on your pitch pipe or piano, and put the block in exactly the right place to make as perfect a C as you can find. Mark where the block is with a pencil, then glue it in place. After you have put the block in place again you can still slide it back and forth a bit to make sure you have a good C before the glue dries. Let it dry for a couple of hours. This new bridge is of course not movable; we call it a "fixed" bridge.

Now let's try another experiment in hearing notes properly. You have set your fixed bridge so that the longer section of the rubber band sounds a C. Find the exact midpoint of this "C" section of the band, using the glued-down ruler as a guide. Touch the string at this point with your fingers or with the ruler you were using for a movable bridge, and pluck it. Now let go of the string and pluck it again. Repeat this experiment a few times. Do you notice anything special about these two notes—the one made with the whole C string and the one made with half of it?

The special thing to notice is that although one note is a lot higher than the other, it somehow sounds "the same." And as a matter of fact, in an important way the two notes *are* the same: they are both C's. We say that they are C's an *octave* apart. The word octave comes from the Latin word for eight. Next time you have a chance, play a note on a white key and then count up or down eight more white keys, with your first key as one:

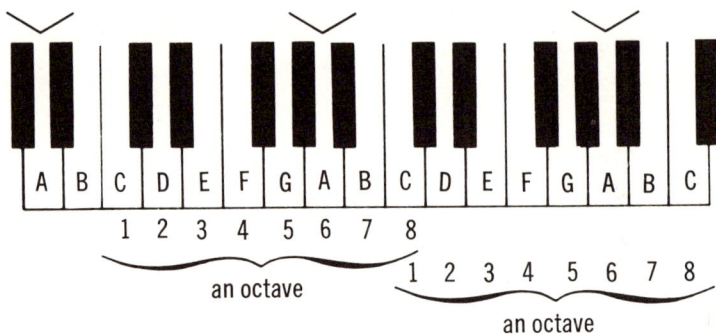

Any time you do this the notes on either end will be an octave apart. Thus, if you find a C and then count up eight notes, you will be playing a C an octave higher. Find an A and count up eight notes, and you will have another A.

But what has dividing the string in half got to do with it? You

40

remember that the shorter the string, the higher the frequency at which it vibrates; and the higher the frequency, the higher the note. When you divide a string in *half* it vibrates at *twice* the frequency. The pitch is "twice" as high—that is, you have an octave. For example, the A shown in the middle of the illustration above has a frequency of 440. The A an octave below it has a frequency of 220, the one an octave above a frequency of 880.

Octaves are one of the most important ways we have of organizing music. They are so important that they are present in the music of most peoples everywhere. For example, even though the music of India sounds very different from ours, they, too, pay special attention to octaves. You can teach yourself to know when octaves are being played if you practice a little. Have somebody play various combinations of two notes on the piano and see if you can guess which ones are the octaves. Once you have learned to hear octaves, you will be able to find the mid-point on your rubber band with your ear alone, without having to check the ruler.

Since an octave has eight notes it is important to know what they are and how they are organized.

The notes running from one end of an octave to the other make up a scale. As you remember, a group of beats make up a measure; in the same way, a group of pitches within an octave make up a scale. There are many different scales in use throughout the world. Some of them, especially those from the Far East, sound quite different from the ones we most often hear.

In our so-called Western music, there are three main scales: the chromatic scale, the major scale, and the minor scale. The chromatic scale is made up of all the black and white notes on the piano between one end of an octave and the next. Go from C to C, striking *all* white and black keys in succession, and you will have played a chromatic scale. The notes in a chromatic scale are an equal distance apart. The chromatic scale is made up of all half-steps:

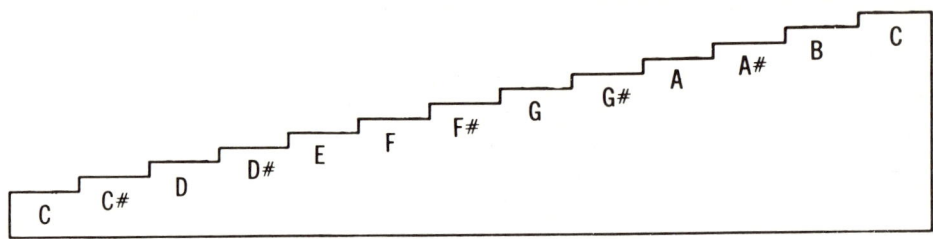

The major and minor scales have only eight notes from one end of the octave to the next. Obviously, they leave out some of the notes in the chromatic scale. In some places the notes skip two half steps at a time, making a whole step. In the major scale there are half steps only between the 3rd and 4th notes and the 7th and 8th notes, like this:

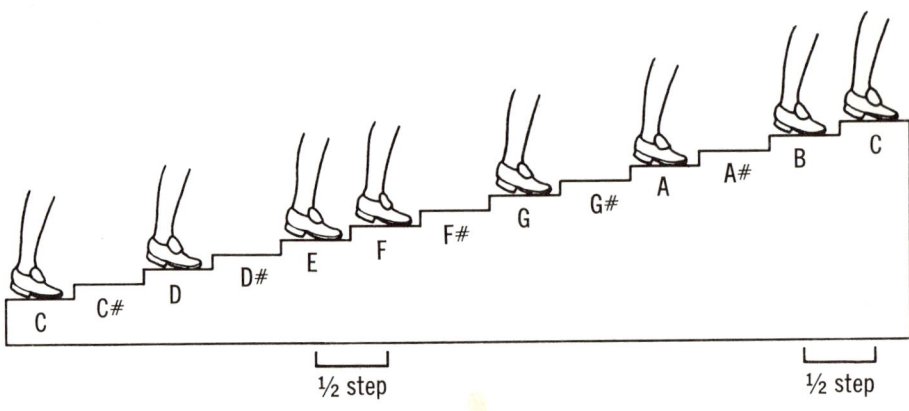

You can begin a major scale on any note, as long as the half steps fall between the 3rd and 4th notes and the 7th and 8th notes. In minor scales, the half steps fall in different places. Learning about the various kinds of minor scales is something you will get when you are further along in your study of music. But just to give you the idea, note that in one of the minor scales the half steps come between the 2nd and 3rd notes, and 5th and 6th notes. On the piano it might look like this:

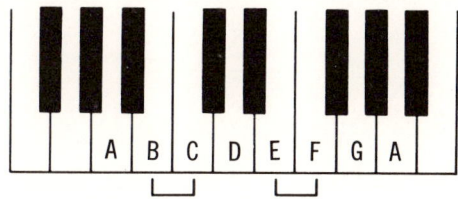

All scales are important but in this book we are going to concentrate on the major scale. Probably you are already familiar with it, because it is the good old do-re-mi-fa-sol-la-ti-do scale you have sung many times. With a little patience you can find a do-re-mi scale on your rubber band. Work on getting do-re-mi first. As you find where they fall, make a mark on your ruler, or on the box. Then get the next notes, until finally you have marked out a complete scale. Remember, the top note in the scale will be an octave above the bottom C—another C.

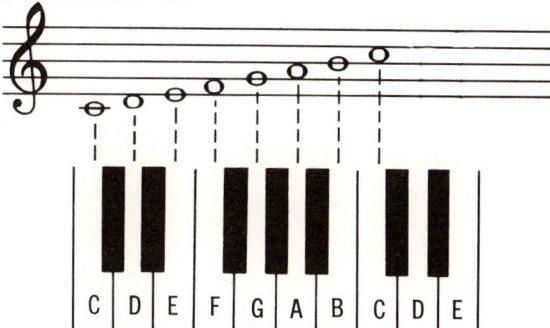

Finding a scale on your rubber band may seem tricky at first, but be patient; once you get started, it comes easier and easier.

Now you have a stringed instrument on which to play tunes. In the next chapter you will learn about reading music in more detail. But just with your ear you ought to be able to play some simple tunes. Try "Frère Jacques" and "Happy Birthday" to begin with. Then see where you can go from there.

6
Writing Melodies

The stringed instrument you learned how to make in the last chapter is a real instrument, perfectly good for playing hundreds of songs on it if you take the time to practice. But you will notice that in one way it is different from the stringed instruments you are familiar with: it has only one string, where violins have four, guitars six, and harps dozens. The violin, and the guitar are pictured on page 55.

One reason for this is that it is easier to play a scale if there is a string for each note, as there is on the harp, because you don't have to worry about getting your fingers or your movable bridge in the right place. But there is another, more important reason. If you have more than one string on your instrument, you can play more than one note at a time. And this brings us to yet another way music is organized—harmony.

Two thousand years ago music was not harmonic. Musicians only played one note at a time to make their melodies. But gradually over a long time they learned to add other notes, until by about four hundred years ago or so they had discovered ways to play many notes at once that sounded well together. As you know, in most of the music you hear today there are almost always several notes being played at the same time.

So let's try it. The first thing you need is two more rubber bands, and two little blocks of wood just slightly higher than the distance between the bands and the box:

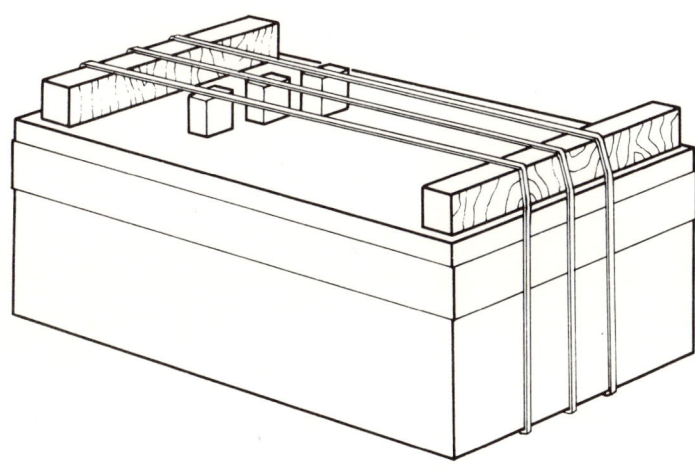

Put the two rubber bands around your box as you did the first one. Try to get your rubber bands fairly close together—not more than an inch apart, and preferably closer to half an inch. Eventually you may want to add more strings to your shoe box and you'll need room.

Now, you are going to tune these two rubber bands to two new notes. But which notes? This brings us back to the theory of music. There's no law, of course, against playing any combination of notes you want. Some modern compositions call for the pianist to smash his hands down on the keys in almost random fashion. But try it yourself; I'm sure you'll find that it doesn't sound very pleasant to you.

Which notes, then, can you play together? Musicians and composers have spent hundreds of years making up rules about this. And they keep changing the rules, too. If you go on to study music some more you will eventually begin learning these rules. But for now, I will give you one basic rule. This rule says if you take every other note from a scale, like the major scale you just learned, you will get a good-sounding combination.

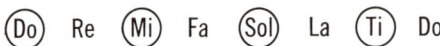

Of course, you only have three strings on your instrument, so you can pick out only three notes from the scale. I am going to suggest that you take the first note, the third note, and the fifth note of the major scale. The reason for choosing this particular combination of notes is that together they make up a major chord. Just as the major scale is the most important one, so, too, the major chords are the most important ones. There is a great deal to be said about chords—how they are made and how they fit together. But for now, just remember that a chord is a certain combination of three or more notes played together. There are dozens upon dozens of combinations which are considered chords under the rules of music theory.

Now, by using your ear, put together your major chord. Think of the song "The Star Spangled Banner." Sing the first few notes. Pay particular attention to the first three notes—the ones that go to the words, "O-oh say." (As you know, there are two notes for the word "Oh," so that it comes out "O-oh.") Those three notes, the very first three notes of "The Star Spangled Banner," make up a major chord.

Use the C that you have already tuned on your shoe box as the third note—the lowest one, the one that goes to the word "say." Tune your two new strings to "O-oh" in the same way that you tuned the C. Slide the blocks of wood under the rubber bands until you have the notes just right, and then glue them down. Before the glue dries adjust them until you have "O-oh say" as perfectly as you can get it. When the blocks are in the right places let the glue dry for a couple of hours or so before you use it. You can pluck it with your fingers, a paperclip or a coin. Of course, you can make melodies on it by playing one note at a time, or you can strum all three notes at once to make a chord.

Now we get back to the subject of musical notation. You learned to notate rhythms in an earlier chapter. Now it is time to discover how to notate pitches as well. That is to say, how do you write down a tune so you can play it the same way the next time?

To begin with, there is the staff:

Each line and each space on the staff stands for a different note. If you put down a scale it will look like this:

As you can see, I've made the scale up of quarter notes, but of course you can use eighth notes or any combination you want. But which line stands for C? Which line for A? It varies. At the beginning of each staff there is usually a symbol, called the clef sign, which tells you. We're going to stick to the treble clef, which uses this sign:

And in the treble clef C is always in the second space from the top and the first line below the staff.

The lines and spaces in the treble clef are named like this:

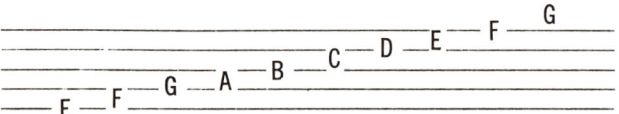

And a C major scale, therefore, looks like this:

As you can see, the top notes of the C scale run right off the clef, but we add little lines, called leger lines, to show where the notes are. Leger lines are like adding a ladder on top of the staff. And, of course, ladders go down as well as up; you can also put leger lines underneath the staff if you want to go below it. As a matter of fact, if you want to write a C scale going down from that C in the middle of the staff, you need a leger line:

Now take a C scale and pick out "The Star Spangled Banner" major chord. Remember, you can make a chord by taking every other note from a scale; and you can make a major chord by taking the first, third and fifth notes from a major scale, like this:

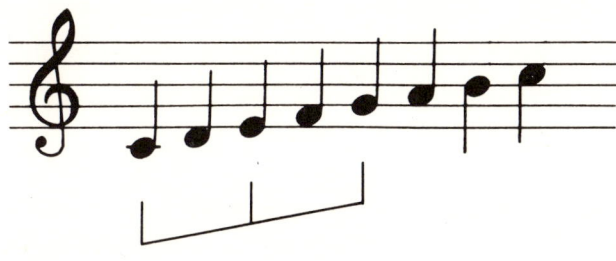

The notes in a C major chord are C, E, and G. They will always be that. So the notes you have put on your shoe-box guitar are C, E, G:

You can now begin to compose some melodies of your own on your shoe-box guitar. Work out some melodies that suit you. You can use eighth notes and rests as well as quarter notes in your melody. Here are two samples:

You can buy staff paper at a music store, but you can also very easily make your own with a ruler. Just remember that there are always five lines the same distance apart in a staff.

In the course of making up melodies of your own, you may have noticed something about your instrument that was not true of the rhythm instruments you made. Most rhythm instruments make only short notes. You can sing a note as long as you want until your breath gives out, but a drum note stops immediately after it gets started. Or, as musicians say, you can "hold" a note with your voice, but a drum can't. And as you have noticed, your shoe-box fiddle can hold a note, too—not as long as you can with your voice, but it can hold a note for a few beats.

Here is how you write down these long notes. If an eighth note gets half a beat, and a quarter note gets a whole beat, what will get two beats? A half note, and here's what it looks like:

𝅗𝅥

And then what comes next? A whole note, which gets four beats, looks like this:

𝅝

So now we have four different kinds of notes:

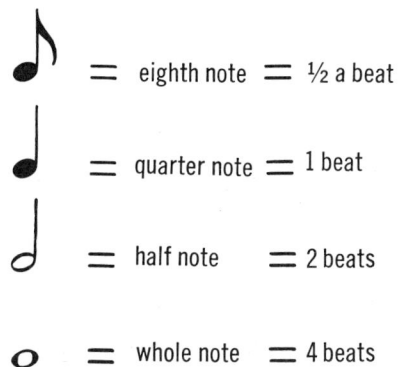

But what about three beats? Or five beats? Or, for that matter, a beat and a half? All of these are easy: you just add two other notes together, and tie them with a curved line, like this:

That curved line, naturally, is called a tie, and these are called "tied notes." A half note and a quarter note add up to three beats; so that is how you write a note three beats long. In the same way you can make up any combination you want. Here are some samples:

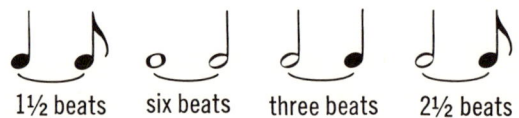

Here is a sample using some of these new notes:

Here's another:

There is even more to be said about these notes. You may remember when I first talked about rhythm, I said that a quarter note could be made to stand for a half a beat or two beats, or almost anything you want. Or to put it the other way around, you can make a quarter note or an eighth note or a half note or many other kinds of notes stand for one beat. It is entirely up to the composer; he can do it any way he wants.

But how do you know which note is supposed to stand for one beat? Right at the beginning of the first staff of music, the composer puts in some numbers to tell you. These numbers are written one on top of the other, like this:

$$\frac{4}{4} \qquad \frac{3}{4} \qquad \frac{6}{8} \qquad \frac{2}{3}$$

These "time signatures," as they are called, are really not so hard to understand. Just remember this rule: the top number tells you how many beats there are in a measure:

$\frac{4}{4}$ = four beats to a measure $\frac{3}{4}$ = three beats to a measure

The bottom number tells you what kind of note gets one beat. A 4 stands for a quarter note, an 8 stands for an eighth note, a 2 stands for a half note, and so forth. The complete rule for time signatures, then, is this: the top number tells you how many beats there are in a measure, the bottom number tells you what kind of note gets one beat:

$\frac{3}{4}$ = three beats to a measure $\frac{2}{2}$ = two beats to a measure
    quarter note gets one beat   a half note gets one beat

Clearly, there are many different kinds of time signatures, and composers today are putting five or seven or three-and-a-half beats in a measure. However, most of the music you ordinarily hear is written in a few basic time signatures. Here are some of them:

Jazz and rock are usually, but not always, played in 4/4. Waltzes are generally written in 3/4. Marches are most often in 2/2 or 2/4—some kind of two-beat-to-a-measure time, because you have only two feet marching. If you plan to learn an instrument you will, of course, learn how to read music in various times, but for now, in order to keep things simple, we are going to stick to those time signatures where a quarter note stands for one beat:

So far you have been playing only one note at a time on your shoebox guitar. However, one of the reasons for making one in the first place was so that you could play a chord. Your C major chord, then, is written with the notes on top of each other, like this:

Sometimes it is interesting to put some chords into your melodies. They often sound especially good at the end:

And, of course, you don't have to play all three notes of the chord; you can play just two of them. Here's one basic idea which sometimes makes an interesting background to sing to:

or

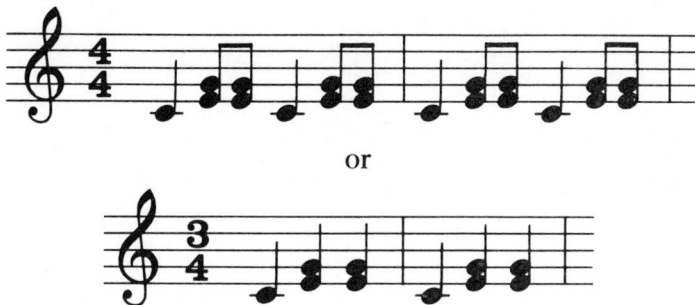

or

Now you have some things to get you started. As you start experimenting you will come up with plenty of ideas of your own.

VIOLIN   GUITAR

7
Making a Guitar—and Chords for It

One very important thing about a band, any kind of band, is that all the instruments should be able to play together. Obviously, if you and your friends are making several shoe-box guitars you want them all to have the same pitch so that they will be in tune with each other. If you use the same size shoe box and the same type of rubber bands for all of them, you can easily get them in tune by sliding the blocks of wood to the right places before you glue them down.

But now we are going to look at yet one more way of organizing music. You have seen that music is divided into beats; and beats can be collected into measures. You have also seen that music is divided into octaves; and that octaves are divided into scales of pitches. You have seen further that pitches can be collected into chords. And now we are about to see that chords can be collected together, too.

The songs in the last chapter were all built on one basic chord, that "Star Spangled Banner" chord we put onto the shoe-box guitar. Actually, very few songs of any kind are based on just one chord. Practically every song you know has at least two chords in it, and most of them more than two. Some songs use dozens of chords. I don't mean that the chords are all played at once; rather, they come along one at a time, so that the first little part of the melody is based on one chord, the next part of the melody on a different chord, and so forth. Usually the song comes back to the first chord again, but not always.

Now that you know how to make a shoe-box guitar it will be a simple matter for you to make more of them with different chords on them. But which chords?

There are a number of different ways to go about selecting notes for chords, but here is a simple rule which will allow you to make seven different chords if you want. That is quite enough to start with. There are hundreds of songs based on only three chords. If you get around to seven you will have plenty.

The rule is this: Starting any place in a scale you like, take every other note. A chord must have three notes in it, but you can take four or five or even more if you want, although I would advise you to stick with three-note chords to begin with. Try it on a piano. Here's the idea:

But as I say, you can start anywhere, like this:

Or this:

The chord you made on your first shoe-box guitar began on the first note of the C major scale; we called it a C major chord. Now I am going to suggest that you make a chord beginning on the *fifth* note of the same scale:

This note is G, and if you take the next two "every other notes" above it like this:

you will have a G chord. As it happens, it is also a major chord—a G major chord.

This chord is an important one because it bears a close relationship to the C chord. As a matter of fact, no matter what major scale you use—a C major scale or an F major scale or a G major scale—the chord that you make by beginning on the first note of the scale and the one that you make by beginning on the fifth note of the same scale are very closely related.

One reason why is that the G chord begins on the same note that the C chord ends on. That is, its bottom note is the same as the top note of the C chord:

You can see immediately a way to make the G major chord. Just make another "Star Spangled Banner" chord on a shoe box, using the top note (G) of your original chord for the bottom note on the new chord. Do it exactly the same way, but tune the bottom note (G) first so that you will be sure that the two chords are in tune with each other.

These chords are called C major and G major, as I have explained. But there is also another set of names for them which it is a good idea to know, because it enables you to discuss the theory of music a little more easily. The chord that begins on the first note of any scale is called "the tonic." The chord that begins on the fifth note of any scale is called "the dominant."

You now have five different notes from which to make melodies. One thing to do is play one part of the melody on one chord, then quickly switch over to the other chord, like this:

You will be able to think up many different melodies of your own.

But as you know, you needn't simply play melodies on your guitars. Guitar players often strum chords as an accompaniment to their singing. The point is to know which chords go with each part of the song. Musicians learn the chords to many hundreds of songs. Actually, when they have had lots of experience, they are usually able to tell what chords go where in a song just by listening to it. You can't do that yet; but with some practice you can learn to do it. For example, probably you know the song called "Merrily We Roll Along." You can play it with just the tonic and dominant chords you have made on the two shoe boxes. (Strictly speaking, there are a couple of other chords that are usually used in this song, but only for a moment and for our purposes can be safely left out.) Sing the song over a few times, and then see if you can figure out where the tonic and dominant chords come. Then, when you have tried it yourself, check and see if you're right:

Guitar Accompaniment for "Merrily We Roll Along"

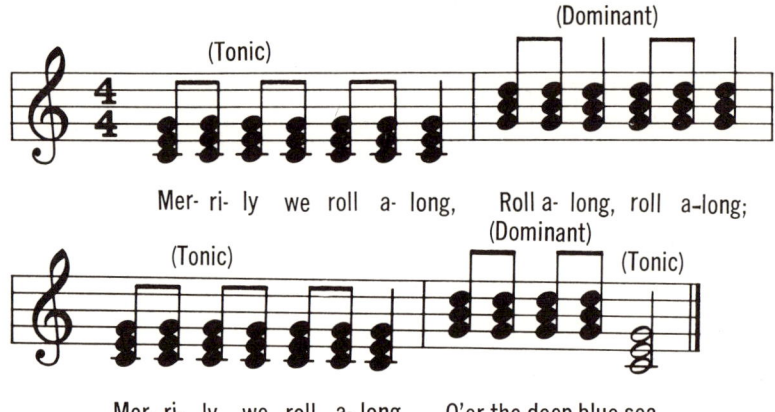

Now try and see how you do with another song you probably know, "The Old Gray Mare."

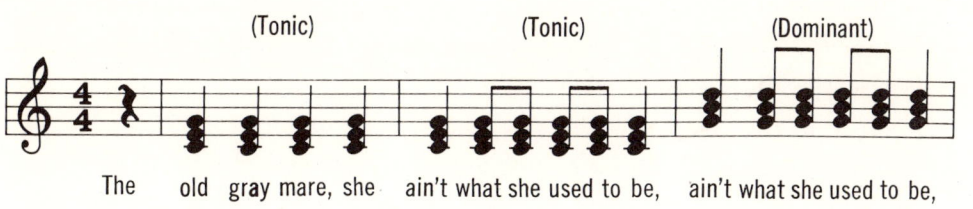

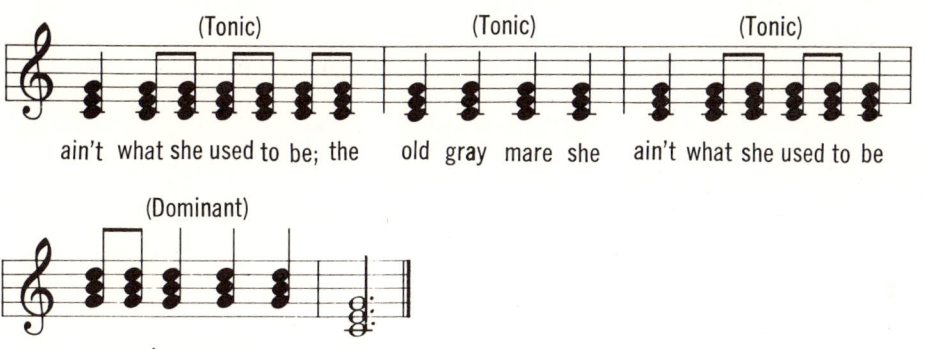

As you can see, with just these two chords, the tonic and the dominant, you can actually accompany yourself on many songs. But if you add just one other chord, you will find that there are really hundreds of songs you will be able to play. This chord is the one built on the fourth note of a scale; in this case, an F:

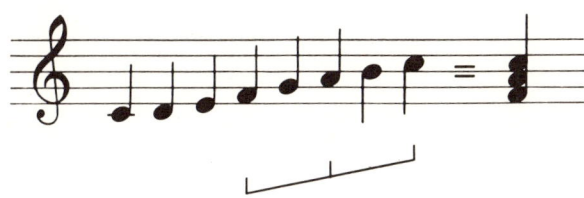

It is called the sub-dominant. "Sub" means "below"—a *subway* is below the ground—and the sub-dominant, as you can see, is just below the dominant:

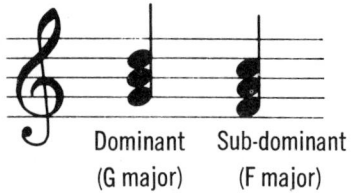

Like both the tonic and the dominant, it is a major, "Star Spangled Banner" chord. There is one other thing about it that you should know: Its top note is the same as the bottom note of the tonic.

This one is going to be a little bit more tricky than making the dominant chord of G. Theoretically you could make it by starting with the bottom note of your C chord, which is C, and making it the top note of your new chord, like this:

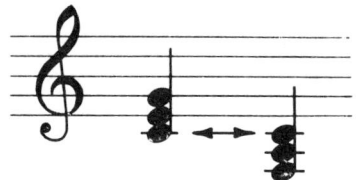

However, you'll find that you can't get the rubber bands to play low enough, unless you use a big box and enormous rubber bands. So what you will have to do is raise the whole F chord up. The clue is the octave. You remember that notes an octave apart are really "the same." Thus, you are going to raise each note in your F chord one octave, like this:

In practice, the way to do it is this: The top note of your F "Star Spangled Banner" chord is C. So tune that note an octave *above* the C at the bottom of your C chord. If you have practiced octaves, you should be able to get it fairly well. Then tune two more rubber bands to the other two "Star Spangled Banner" notes going down, as you have done before.

Now you have three chords.

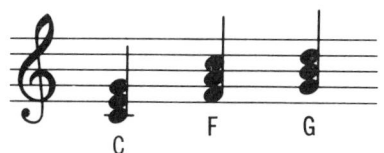

If you spread the notes out in the right order, you will see that they make up a complete scale—in this case a C major scale. (The D above the bottom C is missing, but it appears an octave above as the top note of all:)

These three major chords, the tonic, sub-dominant and dominant—in this case C, F, and G—are strongly related. They make up a kind of little family of chords with the tonic as center. You can easily see why. For one thing, all their notes come from the same scale. For another, each of them shares a note with the tonic chord which helps to tie them together. You will find, as you begin composing songs using these three chords, that you will very often want to begin and end your songs on the tonic. You don't *have* to do this; you should write your songs according to what sounds best to you. Nonetheless, it is very common for songs to begin and end on the tonic. Hundreds and thousands of songs have been written using this family of chords, and most of them use the tonic for beginnings and endings.

You can undoubtedly find some of these songs yourself, but here is one idea to get you started. You may already have heard of "the blues." The blues is a type of song very important in American popular and folk music. It was invented by black musicians at least a hundred years ago. At the beginning, blues singers used their songs mostly to express sadness at the hard lives they had to live as slaves. Today there are happy blues as well as sad ones. In fact, modern singers use the blues to express many different feelings.

When singing a blues, the singer picks out his own melody, either making it up, or using one he has heard someplace. Most often, although not always, the words are made up of one line which is sung twice, and then a final line to finish off the idea. Here is a typical blues:

UNEMPLOYMENT BLUES
© James Lincoln Collier 1973

Not all blues lyrics have that repeated line, but most of them do. Now, even though each singer makes up his own melodies to sing the blues to, almost all of them are based on the same chords. These chords are the tonic, dominant and sub-dominant ones you have learned about. There are certain variations on them that blues singers occasionally put in, but here are the basic blues chords:

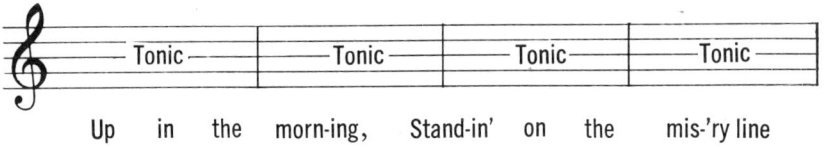

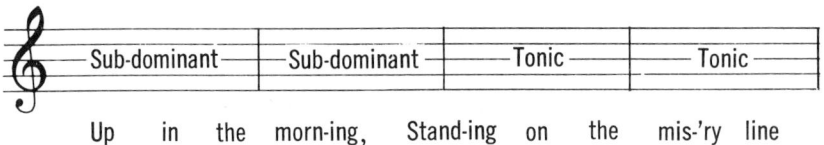

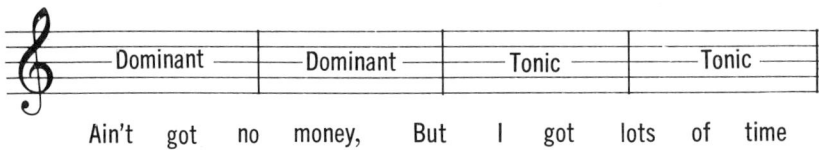

Although the singer will fit in the melody and the words wherever he likes, you can see that it divides rather neatly into three parts, with each of the three lines fitted in over four measures of the music. The guitar accompaniment just goes steadily on "laying down the beat" as musicians say. If you listen to a few blues records you will very quickly get the idea of how it is done. Then you will be able to play and sing the blues yourself.

8
More Chords—and More Strings

Now that you understand the general principle of the shoe-box guitar you can make a whole set of them, big ones and little ones, for the members of your band. You will have trouble finding huge rubber bands for really big ones. The best substitute is to cut a strip from a bicycle inner tube and knot the ends together.

You can use a regular grocery box for a large guitar, but you may find that the pressure of the rubber bands tends to crumple the box a bit. If this happens, reinforce the box inside with a wooden frame, like this:

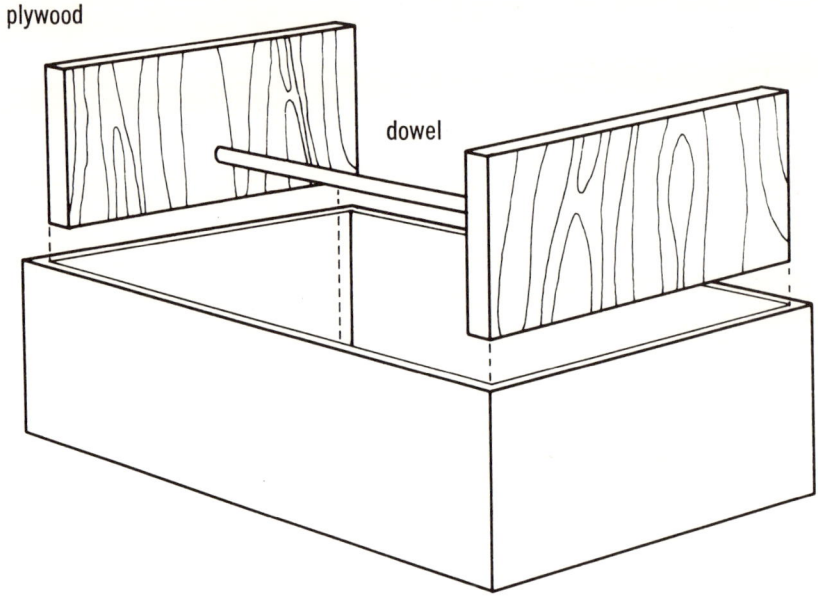

Don't forget to tape up the cracks in the box as you did with the shoe box. Then proceed to tune the strings in the ordinary way. You will undoubtedly want to experiment with various kinds of material to get different sounds. Try metal and wooden boxes as well as cardboard ones.

Here is another experiment worth trying. There is no reason why you can't put all three of your chords—the tonic, dominant and sub-dominant—on one shoe box, like this:

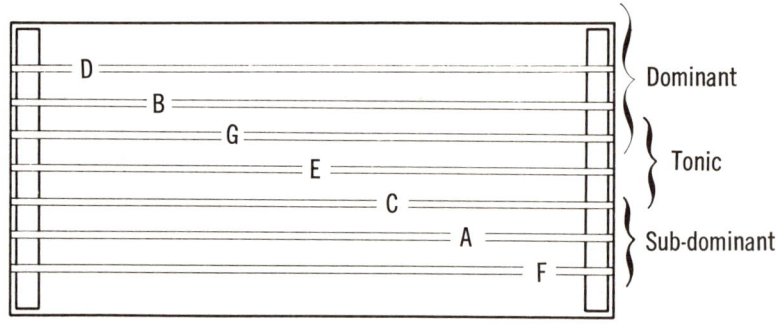

You will notice immediately that because the top and bottom notes of the tonic are found in the other chords you only need seven strings. (Also, you may find that your box needs some reinforcing to counteract the pressure of that many strings.)

And now look what happens: instead of having three chords, you now have five, because you can play a chord using the second, third and fourth strings (A-C-E); and another one using the fourth, fifth and sixth strings (E-G-B):

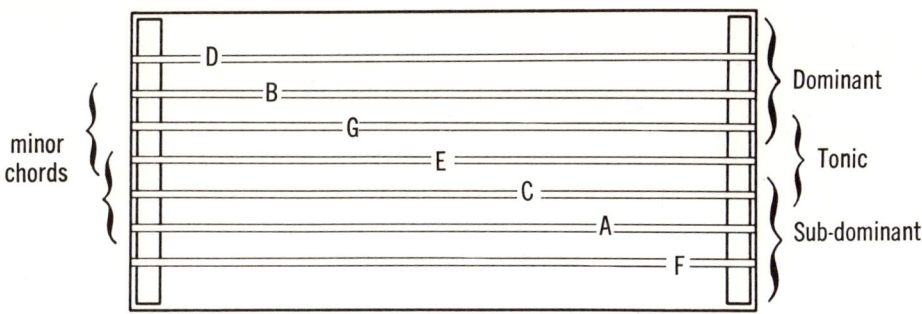

Your ear should tell you something about these two new chords you have just created. Play them a few times, and listen to them. You should be able to tell that they are not major, "Star Spangled Banner" chords. The second note in them is not quite right. As a matter of fact, it is a half step lower than the middle note in a major chord. What is this different type of chord? You're right, it is a minor chord. For now, you might listen to the majors and minors so that your ear learns to hear the difference. A minor chord is somber, even sad. The major chord is clear and bright by comparison.

You remember we discovered that the tonic, dominant and sub-dominant chords together make up a complete scale, if you lower the topmost note an octave. Obviously, then, you can rearrange the strings on your shoe-box guitar so that they go up the scale. It is a good idea to add an eighth string at the top to make a complete scale. This note, of course, will be the C an octave above the bottom C. That is, it is the top "do" of do-re-mi-fa-sol-la-ti-do. You will find it somewhat difficult to play chords on this instrument, because the notes for each chord aren't next to each other. But on the other hand, it is a very good instrument for playing melodies, because the notes are arranged in a scale just as they are on the piano. Try some melodies. If you practice a bit, you'll find that you can pick out all sorts of tunes.

There is one more stringed instrument very commonly found in jug bands which you can make. If you have ever watched a jazz band or a dance band, you have noticed that there usually is a string bass player thumping out the rhythm (there are basses in rock bands, too, but they are electric ones which look and are played like guitars):

You can make what is known as a washtub bass which sounds very much like the real thing. Here's how you do it:

First, you need a metal washtub. A large metal bucket will do, but it's better if you can get a washtub, because it will give a fuller, deeper sound. Next, punch a hole in the bottom just about in the middle. You can do this easily by hammering a nail through it. If you have trouble, make a small hole with a little nail first, then enlarge it with a big nail.

The hole must be big enough for a small bolt to go through. Once you get your hole, put a washer on the bolt, and push the bolt through the hole. If it doesn't go through easily, tap it a few times with a hammer. Then put a washer and a nut on the other end, like this:

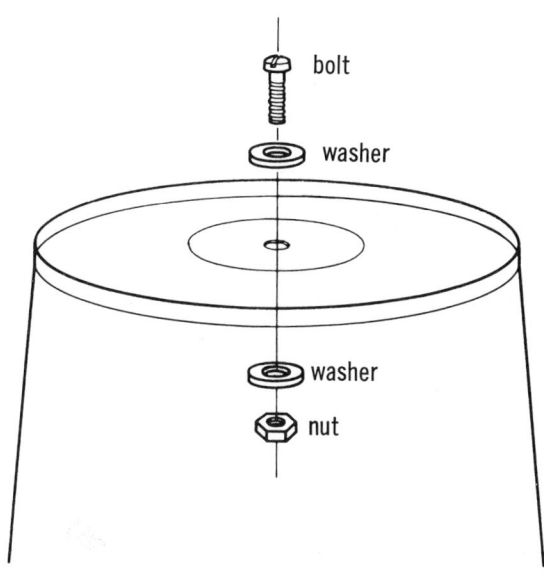

But don't tighten the nut yet. Now you need some sturdy twine, the kind that you use for tying up cartons. A smooth, so-called "polished" twine will be easier on your hands as you play your bass.

Tie one end of the twine around the bolt under the washer. Make sure you have a good knot:

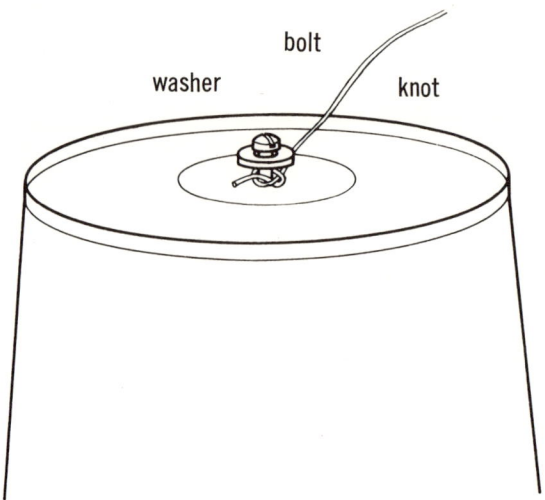

Then when it is firmly tied, tighten up the nut. Your string is now firmly secured to the outside bottom of the washtub.

Next you need a pole of some sort about four feet long. An ordinary mop or broom handle will do nicely. Saw a notch in one end, and a groove going all the way around near the other end:

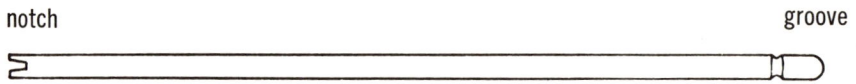

Now fit the notch over the rim of the bucket, and, holding the broomstick upright over the middle of the bucket, tie the twine into the groove in the other end. Get the twine as taut as you can. You will need somebody to help you do this:

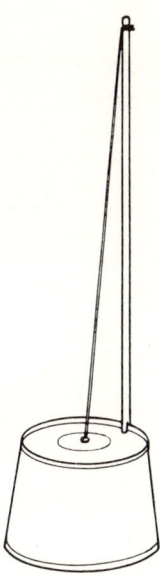

Your washtub bass is now complete. You play it by plucking it. And you can change the pitch simply by pulling the broomstick slightly toward you. This tightens the cord a bit, and as you have already seen, you can raise the pitch of a note by stretching the string:

However, you can also change the pitch by grasping the twine at various places along the broomstick:

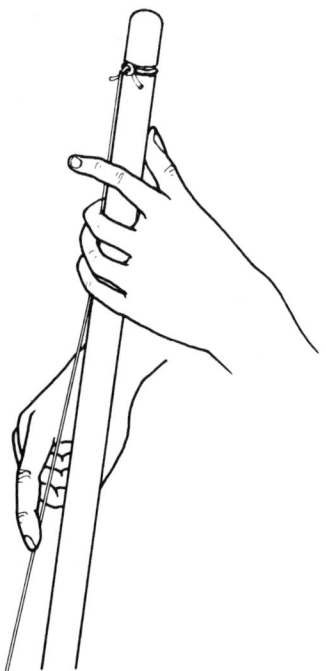

How do you use this new instrument in your band? Generally, the bass player in a jug band or, for that matter, any kind of band, acts as a rhythm-maker along with the drum by plunking out notes on the beat. Unlike the drummer, however, the bass player can play actual notes with their own pitches. This means he has to find notes that somehow fit in with the music that is being played.

The basic rule is to play any of the notes in whatever chord is being played. The simplest thing to do is to play the bottom note of the chord. Have somebody pluck the bottom note on his shoe-box guitar for you, and experiment with your washtub bass to find the note that matches it. If you are using other chords, find the bottom note for them, too. Then, as the band plays along, plunk out the beat, shifting your bass notes with each chord as you go.

Once you have this down, you can try more complicated things. One is to keep alternating between the bottom and the top note of each chord as it comes along. This gives the music more variety:

(Tonic)   (Tonic)   (Dominant)   (Tonic)

Another thing you can do is to play all three notes of your chord one after another, first going up and then coming down, like this:

(Tonic)   (Tonic)   (Dominant)   (Tonic)

But, of course, you don't have to stick to these standard formulas; they are only ideas to help you get started. Once you get some practice on your washtub bass, you will discover that your ear alone will help you find notes to play. You can mix up the chord notes in any way that suits you. In fact, you can mix in notes that aren't part of the chord, as long as you don't put in too many; the chord notes should predominate.

The main point, though, is to use your ear. Practice with your friends, and listen. At first you will have trouble picking out the right notes to play; but in time, if you stick at it, you will find that you really can do it.

You have now made two instruments out of the large family of strings. They are certainly "real" instruments: anything you can make music on is "real." But they are not, as you know, the standard instruments found in most bands and orchestras. They don't sound as well, they aren't as convenient to play, they do not offer as much variety as the standard instruments.

Let's see what some of the differences are. For one thing, in the standard strings a great deal of attention and craftsmanship is given to the wood the resonating boxes are made of, the varnish they are covered with, their shapes and their sizes. It took centuries for musicians to find exactly the best way to make a violin to give it that rich sound and great flexibility. Experiments with types of strings go on today.

For a second thing, stringed instruments are not normally tuned to a certain chord or scale. (The harp is an exception; it is tuned to a scale.) The idea is to tune the strings to a set of notes which will give ease of playing and a broad range.

For a third thing, in all stringed instruments you play many notes on one string. You do this simply by pressing the string against the "finger board" at various places. This is called "stopping" the string. On the guitar, banjo, mandolin and similar instruments, there are little metal bars running across the neck of the instrument which guide the players fingers to the proper notes.

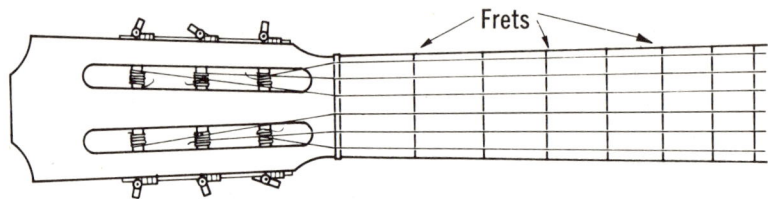

The player presses the string down between these "frets"; the string touches one, shortening the part that vibrates. On violins, violas, 'cellos and stringed basses, there are no frets. The player has to know just by feel where he should press down to get each note. This sounds almost impossible; but in fact even a beginning student learns to do it quite quickly.

Finally, stringed instruments are played in a variety of ways. The piano, which is basically a stringed instrument, sounds when small hammers hit the strings. The strings of a harp are plucked with the fingers. Guitars are plucked either with the fingers or a pick. The strings of violins, violas, 'cellos and string basses are sometimes plucked, but they are usually stroked with a bow. The bow is made of horsehair stretched tightly from one end of a stick to the other. You can get some idea of how this works by "bowing" your shoe-box guitar with a comb. It will work best if the comb is fine-toothed, and if you hold it at an angle to the strings, like this:

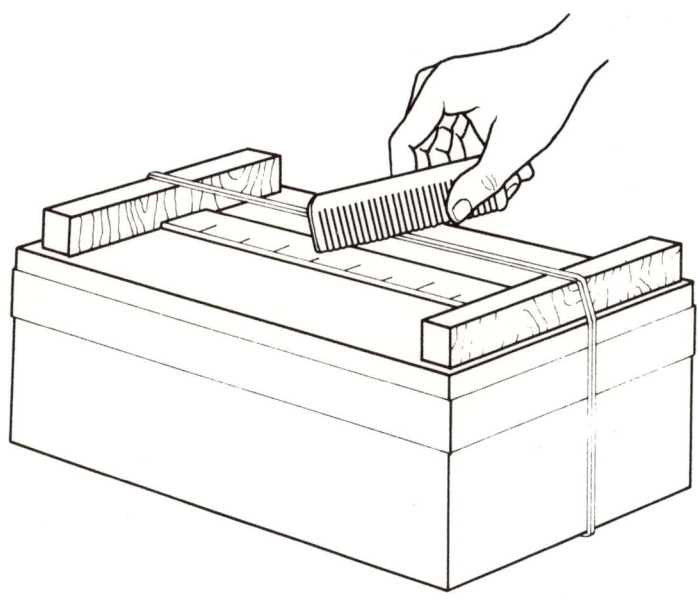

At this point you should probably call your instrument a violin instead of a guitar. You will notice, however, that it is difficult to bow the middle strings of your shoe-box "violin" alone. The real violin gets over this difficulty by having the two middle strings raised, like this:

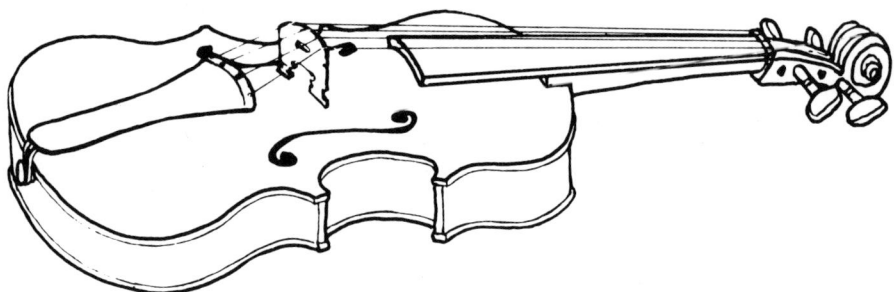

This, of course, makes it difficult to play all four violin strings at once, but expert players have ways of doing it.

If you ever have a chance to try one of the standard family of strings you should certainly do so. In time, if you decide to study music further, you may choose to make one of the instruments from this large family your own.

9
Making Wind Instruments

You have now learned about two of the great families of instruments, the percussion and the strings. The third and last family is the winds. Just as there are many different kinds of stringed and percussion instruments, so are there many kinds of winds. They are divided into two main groups, the brasswinds and the woodwinds, after the kind of material they are made of. The brasswinds include trumpets, trombones, tubas, sousaphones, French horns and a few others. The most important of the woodwinds are clarinets,

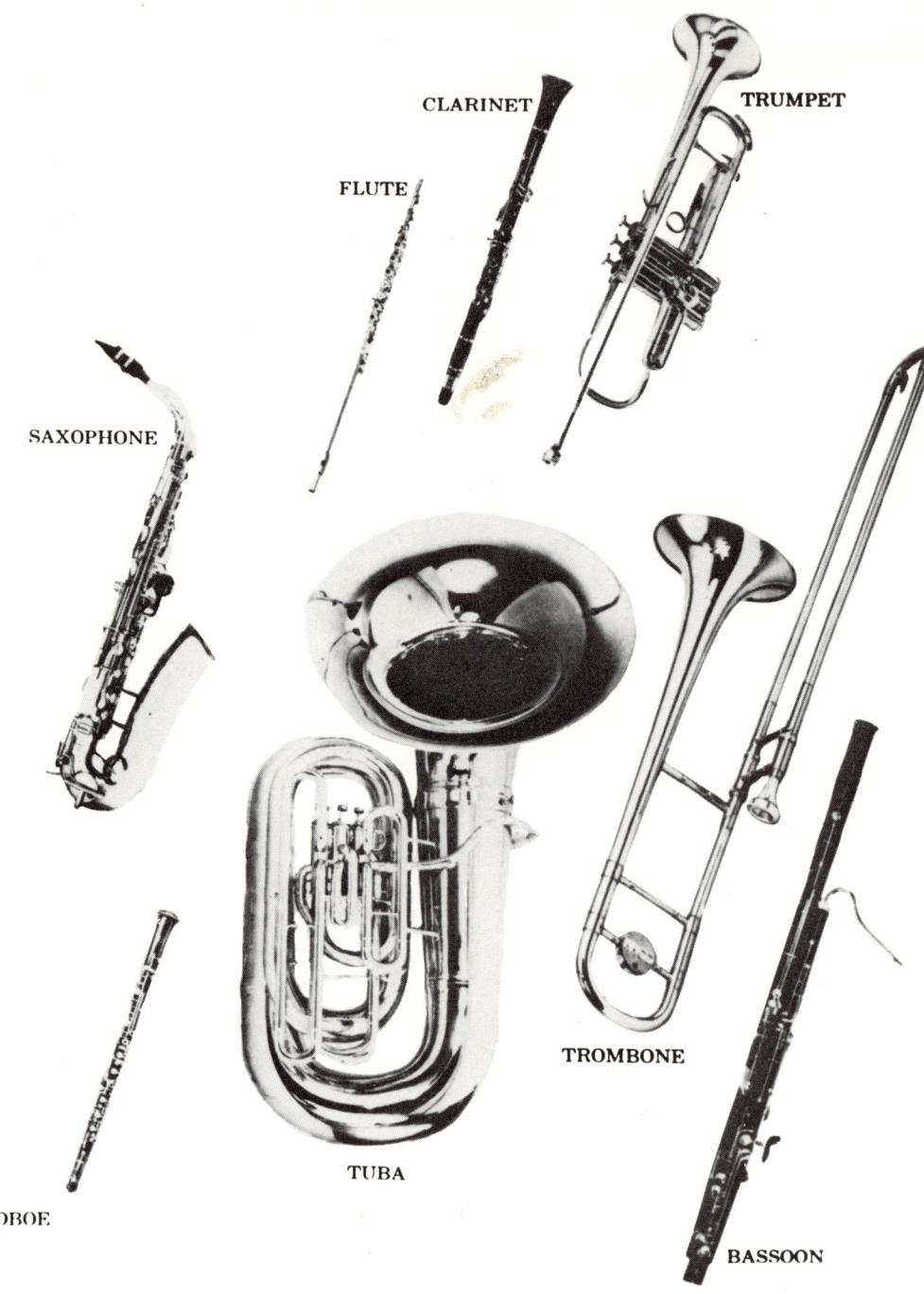

oboes, bassoons, flutes and saxophones. (Actually flutes and saxophones are usually made of metal, not wood, but their sound is closer to the woodwind than the brass sound.)

A stringed instrument makes its sound when a string vibrates. A wind instrument produces its sound by vibrating the column of air inside it. It is easy to understand how a clarinet or a flute contains a column of air. But where is the "column" of air in a trumpet or French horn? Actually, these wind instruments are basically just long pipes that have been curled up or twisted together for convenience. If you unwrapped a French horn it would be about twelve feet long. You can imagine how difficult it would be to march around playing a horn that size. Saxophones, tubas and many other woodwinds are similarly curved to make them easier to handle. Nonetheless, they are all basically containers for columns of air.

You set a string to vibrating by plucking, bowing or striking it. You set a column of air to vibrating by blowing at one end of it. In the brasses, the player sets his lips vibrating by squeezing them tightly together and forcing air between them. The vibrating lips in turn make the column of air in the instrument vibrate. If you like, try it with the end of a short piece of garden hose. You will find it quite difficult to do. It takes a brass player a bit of training to learn how to make his lips vibrate correctly.

In the woodwinds, it is not the player's lips which vibrate, but a thin "reed" made of cane attached to the mouthpiece of the instrument. Air is forced down between the reed and the side of the mouthpiece. The reed is set to vibrating, and in turn the column of air vibrates, too. Clarinets and saxophones are based on this principle.

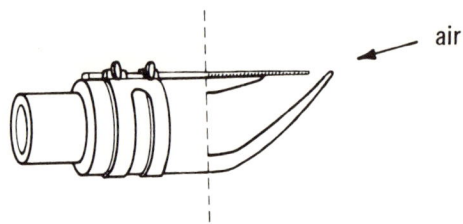

Oboes, bassoons and English horns use two reeds, and are therefore called "double-reed" instruments. Air is forced between the reeds, which begin to vibrate, setting the column of air vibrating.

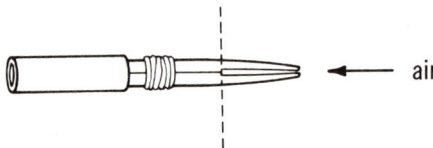

Flutes, piccolos and fifes use yet another principle—one that you will find more useful in making a homemade wind instrument. Here the air is blown *across* a hole. The air itself begins fluttering as it passes over the hole, making the column of air inside the instrument vibrate. The flute is the simplest and oldest type of wind instrument, one you can easily make at home.

To get the idea, you need a bottle. A soft drink bottle is about the right size. Now try blowing across the top of it and see if you can get a sound. You will not find this easy to do at first, but you can learn if you stick with it for a few minutes. The trick is to make sure that you are blowing the air almost directly *across* the top of the hole; do not blow down into the bottle. Your lips will be slightly parted, and the top of the bottle should be about halfway between them so that the stream of air goes across instead of down:

Following our old principle of the bigger the vibrator, the deeper the sound, a big bottle will give you a low note, a small bottle a high one. A jug, obviously, gives you a real bass note, and now you know how jug bands get their name. (Occasionally, a big bottle will surprise you and produce high notes: these are called overtones, but they are too complicated to go into until you have learned more about music.)

You know that you can raise the pitch of a stringed instrument by shortening the string. But how can you possibly shorten a bottle to raise its pitch? Obviously you can't. But you don't need to. The column of air, not the instrument itself, does the bulk of the vibrating, and all you need do to change the pitch of a wind instrument is to shorten the air column. A trombone player does this by moving the slide in and out, actually lengthening the instrument. The valves on a trumpet do the same thing. They are attached to extra pieces of tubing, and when they are pressed down this extra tubing is joined to the main part of the trumpet:

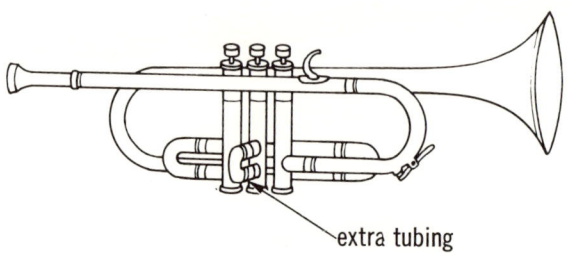
extra tubing

Saxophones, clarinets, oboes and the other woodwinds work on a different principle. To shorten a column of air, you don't have to cut a piece of the instrument off. All you need do is make a hole in the side of it. Wherever the hole is the column of air stops vibrating. Woodwinds have rows of holes in them. They are covered either by the player's fingers or little caps, which can be raised by keys. To "punch a hole" in the side of a woodwind, the player simply presses one of the keys. Wherever the open hole comes the air column ends. Thus, by opening holes near the top he can make the air column very short; by opening only a hole farther down he makes it longer. At any five-and-ten-cent store you can find slide whistles and plastic flutes which will demonstrate these principles.

So, to change the pitch of a bottle-flute, you don't need to shorten the bottle, only the column of air inside it. And you can do that very easily by pouring some water in it. The more water you add, the shorter the air column, and the higher the note will be.

Once you understand this idea you can see immediately the possibilities of making a whole set of bottle flutes with different pitches. You can take three and make a "Star Spangled Banner" major chord. You can make a minor chord. And you can make a whole "do-re-mi" scale on which you can play melodies. Of course, one person can't play a whole lot of bottle flutes. The best idea is to have a different person for each bottle. To play a song you first have to figure out which notes each person plays on his bottle flute. Once everybody learns his part you can really get a nice effect.

Yet it is obviously simpler if you can make some kind of wind instrument which one person can play. Here's the easiest way to do it. First you need some ballpoint pens—one for each note you want to make. Get the kind with a top part which unscrews from the bottom part, like this:

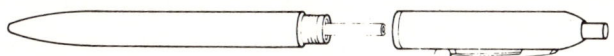

Now take the bottom part. Hold your finger over the tiny hole at the small end and blow across the top, just as you did with the bottle flute. With a bit of practice you should be able to get a tone from it in the same way you did with the bottle. You now have a "ballpoint pen flute," if you want to call it that.

Now, how can we shorten the column of air inside of it? The same way we shortened the column of air inside the bottle flutes—by putting something into it. It doesn't really matter what you put into it—water, dirt, cracker crumbs. The easiest thing to work with, however, is plain old modeling clay. Take a small piece of clay, and roll it into a thin strip which will easily slide into the pen bottom:

Tamp it down inside with a stick of some sort, preferably one with a flat end which won't stick to the clay. A lollipop stick is good. (You may want to wax your stick to keep the clay from adhering to it.) Now when you blow on your flute you will see that the pitch has been raised.

Your job now is to make a set of ballpoint pen flutes. Probably the best idea is to start by making a major chord. For the lowest note, simply use an empty pen. Put a piece of clay around the little end to cover the hole. Tune a second pen by adding clay a bit at a time until you have the pitch right. If you find that you've made the pitch too high by adding too much clay, tamp it down a little tighter with your lollipop stick. If there's still too much, you can push some out the little hole in the bottom with the stick. It takes a good hard shove, but you can do it. Thus, by adding and subtracting you can make your second note. Make the third note the same way. Finally, when you have your notes more or less in tune, you need to mount them on something for convenience. One simple way is simply to wrap the three together with a rubber band, like this:

This way you can play all three notes together to make a chord, although it is hard to make them all play equally loudly, because the note closest to your lips is getting most of the air. You can also play the notes one at a time, just by turning the flute around so that the note you want is against your lips.

Another way of mounting your flutes is to drill holes in a piece of wood and stick the pens through the holes, like this:

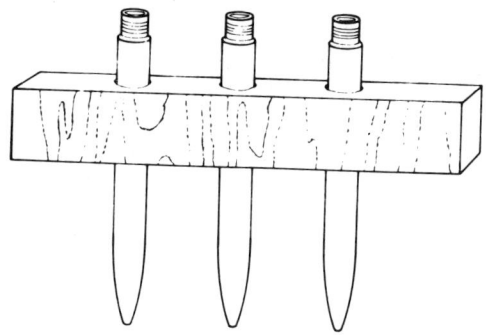

If the pens are a little loose you can either glue them in, or stuff bits of paper or cardboard in beside them to hold them tight. An even simpler thing is just to glue your pens onto a piece of wood or cardboard with regular white glue. And there you've got it.

I have been calling the instrument you have been making a flute. Actually what you have now is generally referred to as "Panpipes," named after the Greek god Pan, who played such an instrument made from hollow reeds.

However, you may have trouble finding ballpoint pens which tune easily to C. Therefore, I suggest one other method of making Panpipes which may prove a little easier. Get hold of some hose. A piece of old garden hose will do, but it is a good idea also to get some smaller ones, too. Your hardware store should have red rubber tubing in assorted sizes. Get a few feet of three-eighths- or one-quarter-inch hose; it is quite cheap. Cut a small piece off the end to make sure that the opening is as close to being perfectly round as possible. Next, twist it four or five inches from the end, like this:

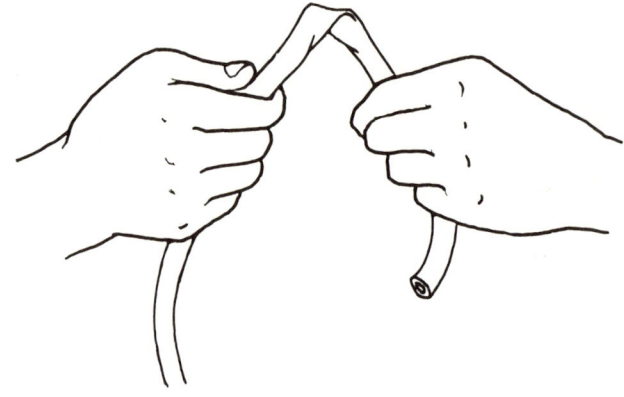

Now blow it as you did your other Panpipes. The note you get should be somewhere near a C. A three-eighths- or one-quarter-inch tube around four and a half inches long will produce an approximate C. With a garden-hose-sized tube you'll need about ten inches to produce a C. Twist your tube at various points until you find your C, more or less. Make sure you make a good tight twist; if there is air escaping from the end you will have a hard time producing a good tone.

Once you have found your C, cut the tube off about a half inch below where the twist came, to give you a little allowance for tuning exactly. Tune the tube with clay as you did the ballpoint pens. It is as simple as that. Using the same technique, you can make sets of rubber hose Panpipes for as many chords or scales as you like. They can be mounted in the same way you mounted your ballpoint pens.

What about writing music for your Panpipes? Clearly, once you have a set tuned, you can write music for it the same way you wrote music for your shoe-box guitar. In fact, you can use that guitar music for your Panpipes if they are tuned to the same notes.

10
Some Other Instruments

How many different kinds of instruments are there in the world? There are around forty basic instruments in common use in the United States today—trumpets, clarinets, organs, pianos, drums and so forth that you are familiar with. But this is only the beginning. There are dozens of lesser-known instruments, like the clavichord, a small version of the piano, which used to be quite popular two hundred years ago, and the mandolin, a stringed instrument something like a banjo, which is not played much anymore. And then there are many more instruments, not much played in America, but which are popular in other countries, like the Scottish bagpipes or the sitar of India. And beyond these there are all sorts of primitive instruments used by tribal peoples throughout history—for example, conch shells which could be blown like horns, or rattles made of dried gourds.

You can see, thus, that by using your imagination you can invent a good many more instruments than there are in this book. Now that you understand the basic principles of music you are ready to move off in any direction you like.

However, there are a few other instruments which you can easily make that you ought to know about. One of the simplest of all is the musical comb. Take an ordinary comb—a fine-toothed one is best—and wrap it with fine paper. Tissue paper will work, but Saran wrap is good and is sturdier. Hold it loosely in your mouth with the tooth end up:

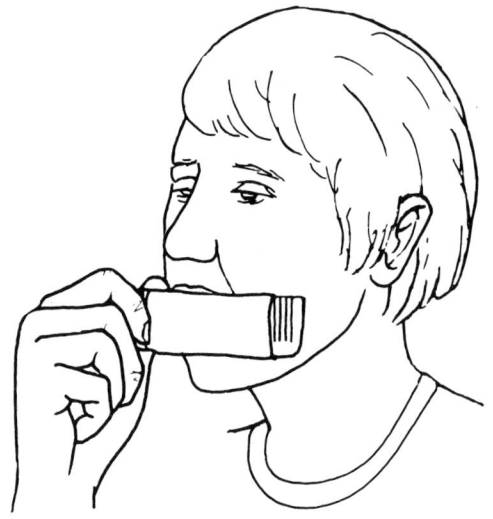

Hum a song and you will produce a buzzing sound. And if you don't believe that music is caused by vibrations, the musical comb will convince you; the buzzing can make the paper vibrate so much it will tickle your lips.

A comb is not a true musical instrument, because it is your hum, and not the comb, which is producing the tone. All the comb does is give it a different kind of instrumental sound. But here is an instrument that is really musical. You need some sturdy glasses and water. By filling the glasses slowly with water and clinking them with a spoon, you can tune them to whatever notes you want. This way you can produce a chord or a scale, if you have enough glasses. It is very easy to tune glasses by putting in more water or tipping some out. Once you get the notes worked out, you can put a crayon mark or piece of tape at the waterline for each glass, so that you can fill them to the same point each time you want to use them. A set of musical glasses is a very useful instrument, because it is quite easy to learn to play a melody on them with a spoon. You can write music for your glasses just as you did for your flute.

Another instrument you might enjoy making, especially if you are artistic, is a maraca. Originally, maracas were dried gourds with seeds or pebbles inside, and handles by which they were shaken. Usually they came in pairs, one for each hand. To make a maraca, first blow up a balloon to about the size of a grapefruit. Cover it with papier maché. (To make papier maché, tear newspaper into strips about an inch wide. Mix some flour and water to make a paste. Soak the paper strips in the paste and lay over the balloon. Let dry.) Next you need a stick or a piece of dowl at least one-fourth of an inch in diameter. Punch two holes in the papier maché at opposite sides of the papier maché balloon, like this:

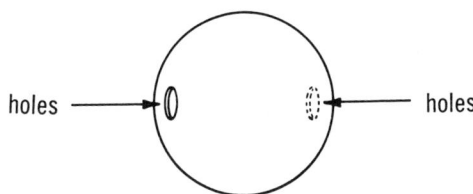

Next pour in your rattlers. There are lots of things you can use: pebbles, dried peas or beans, rice, elbow macaroni—undoubtedly you can think of more. The smaller things like rice will make a light, dry sort of shushing sound; bigger rattles, like pebbles, more of a louder rattling sound. Try a few kinds of rattles before you put the handles on, to see which ones you like best. You may want to put different rattles in each maraca.

To put on the handle, slide it through the holes until it is sticking out of the side of the papier maché, like this:

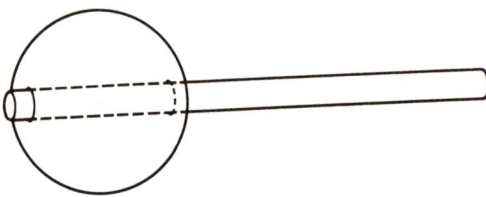

Now glue the stick to the papier maché. When the glue is dry, put more papier maché over the short end, and then cover the rest of the handle to give it a nice shape:

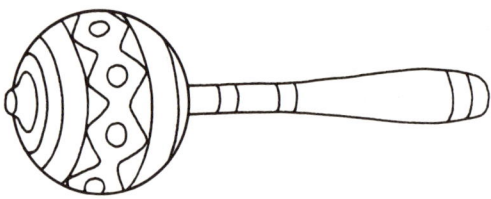

Finally, you can paint it with colors and designs.

Maracas are often used in Latin music—the music from South America. Castanets are also very common in Latin American music. Originally, castanets were two shells tied together in such a way that they could be clicked together to a rhythm. Later on, they were usually made of wood. You can make a pair of castanets very simply out of cardboard and bottle caps. Fold the piece of cardboard in half, and then simply glue two bottle caps to it, like this:

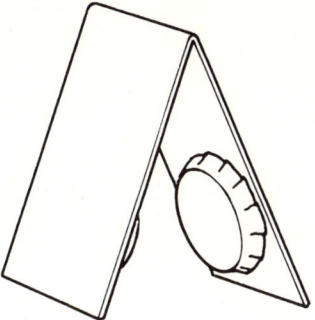

To play it, hold it between your thumb and palm, and click it to the rhythm, like this:

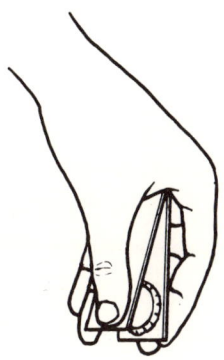

11
The Modern Sound—Electronic Instruments

There is one last sort of instrument I want to talk about which is not really an instrument at all. You remember how all instruments need something to resonate to produce a big sound—the violin string is attached to a wooden box, the piano string to a large sounding board. Until recent times, all musical instruments were made this way. About forty years ago, however, not long after radios were invented, people began to discover that they could increase the volume of an instrument's sound by the use of electric amplifiers. That is, instead of having a wooden or metal resonator, they had an electronic one.

Today the electric amplifier is a common sight in most kinds of popular music. You have certainly seen rock groups standing on a stage knee-deep in huge amplifiers and speakers.

An electric amplifier works just the same way your radio or phonograph works. As you know, a phonograph record is cut with dozens of small grooves going round and round. These grooves look perfectly even, but actually they are filled with invisible wiggles made by the frequency vibrations of the music when it was recorded.

When you play the record, the tiny needle in your record-player begins to vibrate according to the frequency of those wiggles. Of course, the vibrating needle is far too small to make a sound you could hear. However, it sets in motion an electric current which vibrates to the same frequencies; and that electric current runs through the amplifier and is enlarged. (To amplify something means to make it bigger.) Finally, this enlarged electric current, still "vibrating" according to the frequencies on the record, runs into the speakers. Speakers are mainly cones of paper; the electric current vibrates the paper and this produces the sound we hear coming from the record.

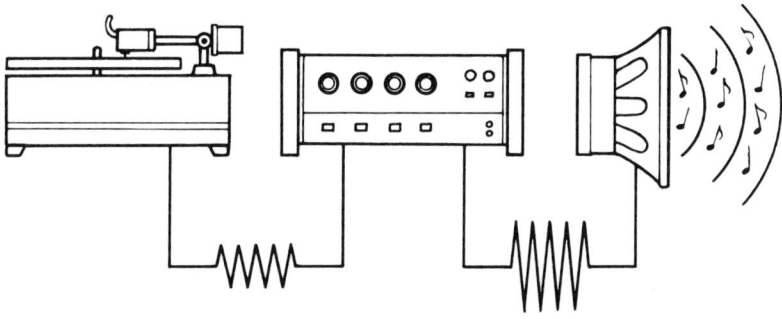

An amplifier works in exactly the same way, except that instead of enlarging the sound from a phonograph needle, it enlarges the sound produced by a musical instrument. The amplified instrument you are most familiar with is undoubtedly the electric guitar. As you already know, on regular guitars, usually called "acoustic" or "folk" guitars, the plucked string makes the wooden body resonate. Although some electric guitars have hollow bodies of this kind, most are merely solid boards with strings attached. Under each string is a tiny "pick-up," which is a kind of simplified microphone. The small sound made by each string is fed into the amplifier, which enlarges it, sometimes to a great volume.

You can make a simple electric guitar of your own. You will have to borrow an amplifier from somebody; or perhaps your school has one. You will also need what is called a "contact mike." You can buy

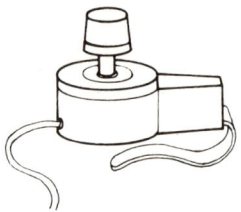

a cheap one at a music store or electronics store for two or three dollars. Anybody who knows a little about amplifiers can show you how to plug in the contact mike.

You are going to make the electric guitar very much as you made the shoe-box one. Take a board about eighteen inches long, and put rubber bands around it.

Under the rubber bands, at each end, slide a bridge and nail it in place:

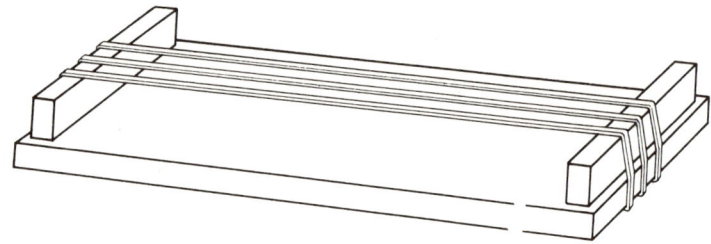

Then, using movable bridges as you did in making your shoe-box guitar, tune your strings to the major chord or a scale, as you choose. Nail the blocks in place. If you leave the nailhead sticking out a little bit, you will be able to loosen the block and move it if your guitar gets out of tune:

Now, attach your contact mike to the fixed bridge at one end. The mike usually is provided with clips for this purpose, but you can tape it on just as well if necessary:

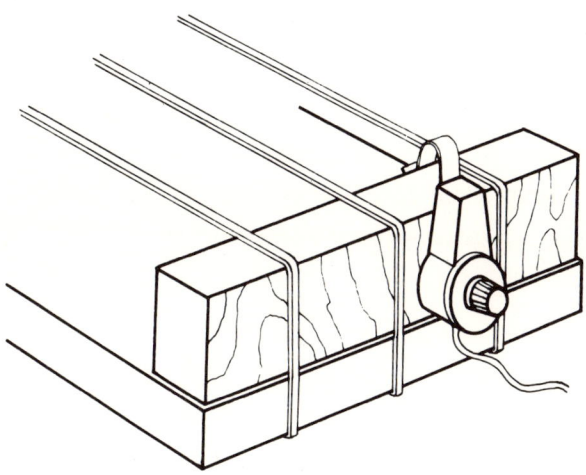

As a matter of fact, you don't really need to build an electric guitar, because you can amplify your shoe-box guitar, if you like. The mike must be attached to the wooden bridge; vibrating rubber bands are too "soft" to work a microphone, and so is cardboard.

You can amplify your washtub bass in the same way. You can attach the contact mike to the string or the washtub, but the best place to attach it is the pole:

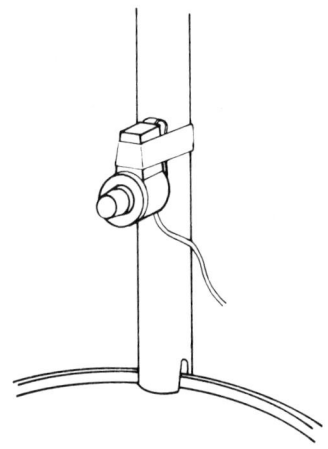

You can also amplify your percussion instruments in the same way. It is a simple matter to clip your contact mike to a pot lid, like this:

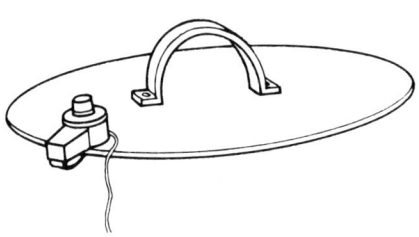

The mike will interfere with the vibrations of the lid slightly, but not much.

You can also amplify your drum by taping the mike to the side, like this:

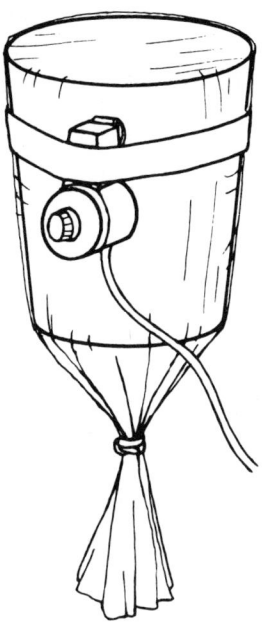

However, the drum should be made of wood, metal or glass; paper or cardboard will not resonate sufficiently to make the mike work.

Similarly, you can put mikes on your water glasses, if you want. They should be taped to the bottom of the glass, though; otherwise the clip interferes with the vibrations of the glass too much. This means that the glasses will have to stand up on something like blocks of wood:

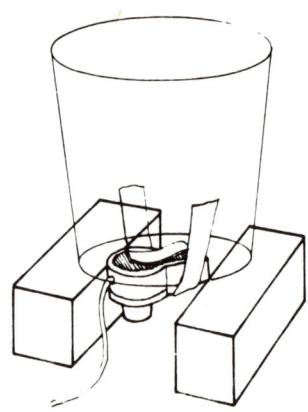

Actually, the best way to amplify something like your musical glasses is with a regular microphone. You can buy a microphone for around ten dollars, but make sure that it will work with the kind of amplifier you have. The person who showed you how to work the amplifier can help you plug in the mike. Sometimes, if you place the microphone too close to the amplifier, or turn it up too loud, you will get "feedback"—a shrill sound coming out of the amplifier. You will want some help to learn how to manage this.

In any case, you can use a microphone to amplify your Panpipes, water glasses and entire band, if you like, although to do that you will probably need three or four mikes and two amplifiers. Experiment; try both your contact mike and your regular mike on various of your instruments to find out which combinations work the best. If you have enough microphones you can make a band out of one bass, one homemade electric guitar, one set of percussion and a set of water glasses.

12
Putting Your Jug Band Together

At this point you should be ready to put your jug band together. You know how to read music a bit, you know how to work out rhythms to songs, and you know something about chords. Now how are you going to organize it all?

I suggest that you divide your group into three sections. First, there is the rhythm section made up of the percussion instruments and the washtub bass. The job of the rhythm section is to "lay down a steady beat" as a foundation to support the rest of the instruments. It is a little like making a floor on which the chords and melodies can stand. Now, of course, everybody in the rhythm section can't simply play whatever comes into his head; it would all get too jangly and nobody would have a very clear idea of where the beat was. It is necessary to organize things a bit, so that perhaps the cymbals and rattles are playing one kind of beat and the drums another. If you get too many different kinds of beats going at once you will have difficulty keeping them in your mind and might be thrown off.

The second section is made up of the chord instruments, especially the shoe-box guitars. They should play a very simple rhythm too, so as not to complicate things. Their job, of course, is to supply the harmonies that go with the song.

Finally, there are the melody instruments, such as the water glasses, Panpipes, and any guitars you have made with a full scale on them.

Actually, there is no law against adding a few real instruments to your jug band, if you want. Perhaps somebody is learning the guitar and can play melodies on it; perhaps you have somebody who can play the piano or a melody instrument like the clarinet, which might fit in. There is no reason why you shouldn't add some of these instruments if you want, but, of course, you are beginning to get away from the idea of a jug band when you do.

At first, you are going to find it difficult to work up songs so begin with simple ones. Divide the group into its three sections and have them practice separately. The people playing the melody instruments will learn the tune, and the rhythm instruments will work out interesting beats that fit well with the song. The chord instruments have the hardest job—figuring out which chords fit with the melody. At first, you may need some help with this. Your teacher, or older brother or sister who knows something about music should be able to help you work out the right chords. The washtub-bass player also must find right notes to play, but probably he can do this by listening sharply to the tune and experimenting with various notes until he gets the right ones.

One other problem that concerns you is keys. Because all of your instruments are in the key of C, you will have to "transpose" all songs into that key. To transpose means to change a song from one key into another. There is an easy way to do this. First play a C major chord (the tonic chord) on your shoe-box guitar a few times, and then begin singing the song to it. In the simple songs you are going to be learning to play, the first note of the song will almost always be one of the three notes in that C major chord. Your ear will quickly tell you which one. Once you have the first note, it will be easy to sing the rest of the tune, and then learn to play it on your various melody instruments.

So now you are ready to start. Actually, you have already started, because you have learned parts of some songs, and a good many rhythms. You should be able to compose your own songs, too. But in order to give you a bit of help, on the next few pages you will find five songs worked out for your jug band. Each player may copy out his own part for convenience. That way he may take his music home to practice it. Good luck, and have fun.

Appendix: Music for Your Jug Band

HAPPY BIRTHDAY

JINGLE BELLS

DECK THE HALLS

TURKEY BLUES

© James Lincoln Collier 1973

110

FROGTOWN ROCK

© Geoffrey Lincoln Collier 1973

Index

amplifier, 94-100

bagpipes, 89
balalaika, 32
ballpoint-pen flute, 85-88
banjo, 32, 76, 89
bar, 19
   see also measure
beat, 6, 14, 15
bottle flute, 82-84
black musicians, 64
blues, 32, 64
blues lyrics, 65
blues singers, 64
bow (violin) 77
bowstring, 32
brasswinds, 79

castanets, 92-93
'cello, 32, 76, 77
   see also violincello
chords, Chapters VII, VIII;
   47, 102

major chord, 46, 54, 58, 84
minor chord, 84
chromatic scale, 41-42
clarinet, 32, 79, 83, 102
clavichord, 89
clef sign, 48
contact microphone, 95-100
cymbals, 8, 17, 18, 23, 102

dance band, 70
"Deck the Halls," 109
dominant chord, 59, 60, 61, 63, 65, 68
double-reed instruments, 82
drums, 10, 11, 12, 16, 17, 18, 32,
   74, 98-99, 102
drumheads, 11
drum sets, 7

ear training, 39
eighth note, 23-27, 48, 50, 51, 52
eighth rest, 24-27
electric amplifier, 94
electric guitar, 95-97

fife, 82
finger board, 76
fixed bridge, 40
flats, 38
flute, 32, 79, 82, 84-88
folk music, 32
frequency, 30, 41
frequency vibrations, 94
French horn, 79, 81
frets, 77
"Frogtown Rock," 111

guitars, 1, 44, 56, 76, 77, 95, 102

half note, 51, 52
half step, 42
"Happy Birthday," 107
harmonica, 1
harmony, 45
harp, 44, 76, 77
horns, 90

jazz, 19, 23, 26, 32, 53
"Jingle Bells," 108
jug bands, 2, 70, 74, 83, 102, 103

kettledrums, 7

leger lines, 49

mandolin, 32, 76, 89
maraca, 91-92
marches, 53
measure, 19, 20
  see also bar
melody, 5, 59, 60
microphone, 95-100

moveable bridge, 36, 38
musical comb, 90
musical notation, 13, 47

note, 2

oboe, 79, 84
octave, 40, 41, 43, 62, 63

Pan pipe, 85-88, 99, 102
percussion instruments, 6, 12, 98
piano, 1, 32, 37, 39, 41, 57, 77, 102
piccolo, 82
pitch, 29-31, 37, 83
pitch pipe, 39

quarter note, 14, 15, 16, 26, 27, 48, 50, 51, 54
quarter rest, 15, 16, 26

rattle, 90-92, 102
resonance, 10-12, 32, 76, 93-94
rests, 15
rhythm, 5, 6
rhythm band, 13
rhythm section, 101
rock, 26, 32, 53

saxophone, 79, 81, 84
scales, 41-43, 48, 76
  major scale, 41-43, 46, 49, 58, 63, 69
  minor scale, 41-42, 69
scraper, 9
shakers, 8
sharps, 38
shoe-box guitar, 67, 69, 77, 97, 102

sitar, 32, 89
sixteenth note, 26
slide whistles, 84
speakers, 94
sound, 3
sousaphone, 79
staff, 47-50
string, 10, 11, 32, 76, 77
string bass, 32, 70, 76, 77
string family, 32
strong beats, 21-22, 25
sub-dominant chord, 62, 63, 65, 68
syncopation, 26

tambourine, 8
tempo marking, 15
tempo, 15
thirty-second notes, 27
tied notes, 52
time signatures, 53-54
tonic chord, 59, 60, 61, 63, 65, 68, 69
tone, 2
transposition, 102-3

treble clef, 48
triangle, 8
trombone, 79, 83
trumpet, 32, 79, 83
tuba, 32, 79, 81
"Turkey Blues," 110

ukelele, 32

vibration, 3-6, 10, 29, 81-84, 94
viola, 32, 76, 77
violin, 32, 44, 76, 77
violincello, 32
   see also 'cello

waltzes, 53
washtub bass, 71-75, 97, 102
water glasses, 90, 99, 102
weak beats, 22-23, 25
whistle, 30
whole note, 51
whole step, 42
wind instruments, 1, 79
woodwinds, 79, 84

ABOUT THE AUTHOR

JAMES LINCOLN COLLIER, author of many children's books, is a former professional musician who has played in jazz and dance bands as well as chamber music groups. He is founder of the Hudson Valley Brass Ensemble, and a publisher of music through Conservatory Publications. His previous books on music for children are *Practical Music Theory; Which Musical Instrument Shall I Play?;* and *Inside Jazz.*